MASON JARS...
CLOSING THE LID ON
THE LAST
OF
THE NINES

HUMOROUS ESSAYS ABOUT THE 90s

JOE MASON

MASON JARS...
CLOSING THE LID ON
THE LAST
OF
THE NINES

HUMOROUS ESSAYS ABOUT THE 90s

JOE MASON

Copyright © 2003
All Rights Reserved

PUBLISHED BY:
BRENTWOOD CHRISTIAN PRESS
4000 BEALLWOOD AVENUE
COLUMBUS, GEORGIA 31904

Dedicated to Lisa And Scott,
Both of whom are equally "special."

Acknowledgements

To my wife, Virginia, for her support,
suggestions, and editing.

and

To R. Denny Spear of Dunwoody, Georgia,
Minister, Artist, and Friend for all Seasons,
For the cover design

PREFACE

As the last decade of the last millennium commenced, I found myself musing more and more, albeit somewhat slovenly, about what I would do when the 90s came to a conclusion...as in, fini...kaput!

Actually, I had been thinking about this off and on for years, but when 1990 hit, I began to have a tinge of inner revelry, realizing that in just 10 short years - when the year of our Lord, number 2000, burst on the scene, regardless of Y2K - it would be the precise time when I could valiantly act upon the concept which our fellow citizens began to embrace some 65 or more years ago. I could quit work and get free money!

You may remember that this was about the time of the onset - or what some would call the onslaught, depending on your political bent, your pocket book, and your age - of the "Great Perpetual Pilfering of the Populace' Paycheck," circa 1935, lovingly referred to as the "Social Security Act." From that day to this, men and women alike have thought and planned for that utopian dream called *retirement*. Except for the "Gen Xer's." They, of course, wonder how the heck they will pay the billions for the baby boomer's double S. But that's their problem. Mine was getting safely through the 90s.

What most of us envision it to be is a bodacious, journeys-end concept toward which we worked, yea, even slaved, saved, raved, and craved. Finally, we would receive the monthly paycheck we had worked and saved for...free money! It would become our "rite of passage" toward freedom of time, choice, and mobility, enabling the retiree to experience the unencumbered exhilaration of the open road, the sunny beaches, or the sit-back-and-do-nothing rocking chairs.

So, I knew that if I could just make it through the 90s, I could hit the road or I could rock, baby, rock. As the honorable Capt. Al Buckler of Avondale would say, in the words of the late New York Yankees announcer, Mel Allen,..."Hot diggity dog!"

I realize not everyone wants to retire. In fact, my father may be "spinning in his grave" at the thought of his son's slothfulness.

4

He was a straight, resolute individual who never wavered from an ingrained work ethic which he accepted early on, I believe, and continued to genuinely express all of his adult life as his noble destiny of purpose.

He labored in a tenacious manner for most of his 76 years, only to die, sadly, a year after being "forced to retire" – a phrase which can become an infamous death warrant to some. I believe he "lost his way," and, forced from his comfortable place of "work-purpose," could not recover and possibly missed the splendid opportunities which retirement can bring.

My dad was no different than others who retire from their noble destiny called work. They may spend an inordinate amount of time looking back, pondering the losses of friends and family, and lamenting over their ailments and illnesses. Lacking the will power to redirect, reapply, relearn, and thus, harness the positive aspect of our retirement time "gift," can cause life's grains of sand to swiftly slip through one's fingers, never to be recovered.

But alas, it is not my purpose here to become too serious about retirement. There is an upside and a downside to the concept, to be sure. My son played drums in a band for some years and one of his albums had a song entitled "Don't Let It Take You Over." If we give into the "lamentations" of our retirement, they might take us over and our spirits can shrivel like, well, the sadly unglamorous prune. Prune, you ask?

Well, yes. When the 90s began, I started eating more prunes and soon noticed right off, a vertical line down the side of my nose. Looked like the beginning of the dreaded "prune face syndrome," which I will address later in this book. Am I going to retire with *this?* I wondered. But there was more

I dealt with more government tax brackets, surveys misusing my name, the dreaded yellow pollen, the Olympics are coming-the Olympics are coming, trying to remember what I forgot, trying to change habits at this age, and coming to grips with life being more and more like a "box of choc-lates, never knowing what you're gonna get."

5

I didn't want the issues of the 90s to "wrinkle up" the possibility of my grand march toward 2000, and retirement. Some of my younger compatriots would agree among themselves, of course, that I don't really have enough wrinkles to *look* like a prune, but would hasten to add that I may be *"full* of prunes." The very idea.

I suppose that you, the reader, might think the same, but I will trust your good judgment. Many of you would recognize that, as in the two previous "Mason Jar" books, a good portion of the musings herein are from articles that I wrote while "employed" (boy, if you could have seen my monthly paychecks!) as a weekly writer for the Decatur/Dekalb (Ga) News Era. The essays have to do with the life and times of the 90s which you may happily recall and hopefully, will bring a smile, or memory of a similar journey as mine.

By the way, when 2000 came, I did "hang it up" at the First Baptist Church of Decatur after 21 years, and am struggling to do all the things I want to do. I had always heard that when you retire, you never have enough time and I'm finding that to be true. But I finally finished this book. Now, there's one more word before "closing the lid."

I'm not sure if historians have made a suggestion of the most politically correct, descriptive adjective for the last decade of the century as yet. I have yet to hear one posed. Of course, I could argue that this current decade is literally the last decade of this past century, even though the 1900s were the 20th century and the "twenty hundreds" are the 21st century. But why be technical and mess up a good thing...like this book!

The 1890s were called the "gay nineties" but I doubt that we could say the same about the 1990s and be, uh, that all-inclusive. Maybe the "talking nineties." Seems like all we did was talk more and more – radio, TV, conventions, cell phones – whole lot of talk transpired. We could call them the "good old 90s," but the Republicans might argue that they weren't so good for them, while others would say that associating with anything old is discriminating or that it makes light of those who are, say, in their nineties while living in the nineties. Political correctness is a booger, isn't it?

So, I'm inclined to say the appropriate adjective is not really an adjective, but sort of an expression. The last decade is about what I would call…*the "last of the nines"*…realizing, of course, that there are no more "90s" for almost one hundred years! No more 19's, forever! Zilch. Nada. These 90s are "gone with the wind." Now, there's a catchy expression.

Joe Mason

INTRODUCTION

There are two expressions which we use from time to time when an event or episode happens to take place, causing us to roll our eyes around, or at least give a "goooolleeeee" longer than ole Gomer Pyle ever expressed. And the winners are... *"what goes around, comes around,"* and *"the more things change, the more they stay the same."* They come to mind when I think of how the 90s began.

In the year of 1990, the following news items were in the forefront:

- A prominent bishop of the Catholic church in Atlanta was in scandalous hot water for some sexual impropriety with a woman, which ultimately caused his dismissal and implicated others of the cloth as well. The beginning of the next decade, as we now know, didn't bode well for Catholic Clergy, either.

- In 1990 the Georgia Gubernatorial race, was won by none other than Mr. Zell "Zig-Zag" Miller. Early on, in this current decade, he still holds forth with the nickname, "Zig-zag," this time as a democratic senator in Washington, who has, on occasion, made his republican leaders happy, too. But now he says he is calling it quits. We'll see. Could be he's "zigging...or zagging."

- In June of 1990, the cover of *U.S. News & World Report* featured "The Most Dangerous Man In The World," a caption under the picture of Saddam Hussein. At the beginning of the 21st century, he was still in power and people wondered if, as Lewis Grizzard used to say, he was still "up to somethin.'" (Latest update: Now, we just want to know where he is)

- In 1990, the President of These United States was George H. W. Bush. Ten years or so later, the President of These United States is George "Just W." Bush, touching off what may become a "family tradition." There are other Bushes out there, friends, - brothers, nephews, and even a couple

8

of female Bush twins…who knows? One day you might hear a commercial on television, with two lovely girls doing the two-step arm in arm, while singing…

"Double your pleasure, double your fun,
We're running for President, you get two for one."

You heard it here first, folks, from Josephus!

PART I

FOR THIS "AVERAGE JOE," PLANTING OKRA IS NOT A GOOD WAY TO SPEND THE SPRINGTIME

THE PURPOSE OF SPRINGTIME

"To everything there is a season, and a time to every purpose under the heaven" Ecclesiastes 3:1 (KJV)

In addition to the above quote from the Bible, there is a line attributed to some wag, to wit, "In the springtime, a young man's fancy turns to what the women have been thinking about all winter." This, of course, is after the basketball season. Like many of my gender, I have known this for more years than I care to mention. I think it all began during the ripe old age of 14 when I started talking in complete sentences to a girl named Peggy Sue and soon became disinterested in riding my bicycle to school with my buddy, "Fig" Newton Moore, who became commander in the Navy while I continued to struggle with speaking to the opposite sex coherently.

Something was definitely in the air in the spring of those early 50s, as well as honeysuckle and Old Spice. The only complicated issue I had to deal with was the constant frustration of juggling my time between my cuddly cutie – whomever she was at the time – and Miss Dorothy's Spanish conjugation or Miss Juanita's geometric theorem.

(In those days, we could actually call some teachers by their first name, I suppose because they were single and all they had to think about through the winter, poor lasses, was Spanish quizzes and Geometry angles.)

I have had other springtime diversions I won't go into and one or two I wish I could forget, like, when I was 17, "it was a very good year," as Mr. Sinatra used to sing.

Well, the spring air was laced with the sweet aroma of Kentucky bluegrass, but when summer came, my father took the family – which was me and Mama - to Utah on business and when I returned home, the "good year's" aroma had gone sour. Out of sight, out of mind, I think is what she said.

Ah, but that was decades and a couple of lifetimes ago. When the first spring of the 90s came along, there was much more than mere feminine, wintertime fantasies to occupy our minds. The

Braves were still in a disaster mode with the late Jim "Hey, Vern" Varney as a mascot of sorts; the NCAA Final Four had the first-time Arkansas Hogs playing which caused the people in Big Blue Kentucky country a huge depression; there was what some southerners thought was a "pirated" version of Scarlett O'Hara's next adventure; and, true to form, we were covered with the yellow pollen once again.

All these things impinge upon spring's "young man's fancies," to say nothing of wintertime girl-thought trying to express itself, and keep us from thinking about God's true intention for the creation of that special time of year.

Well, one morning in early April of 1990, I walked out of that notable eatery of Decatur, Evans Fine Foods, where "everybody knows your name," and there on the sidewalk, springtime was flourishing. A young couple who had walked out a few moments before me, having finished their eggs and toast, were now having their morning "dessert." They were locked in a springtime, been-thinking-about-all-winter embrace/kiss that would make your toenails curl up inside your SAS shoes.

I walked by, eyes dead ahead, and said, "Now that's the way to start a Monday morning!" She paused to giggle slightly, and he paused to catch his breath, smiled, and resumed their mutual grasp. I guess you could say that his springtime fancy and her wintertime thoughts expanded into "kissing coagulation," right there on the sidewalk.

And that, friends, is exactly what spring was created for. Oh, I realize that people in my adopted state of Georgia think is was created for the Masters, and people in my native state of Kentucky think it was created for the Derby. Wrong on both counts.

So, my suggestion for every springtime is that you find your favorite love-person and present the gift of a slurpy kiss and holy hug that will last until the first frost! Do you reckon this is one idea Solomon had in mind in Ecclesiastes?

WHY NOT USE HORACE OR CARL FOR THE "AVERAGE GUY?"

There was a report which came out in the early 90s about a "Joe Average" study. One day, I woke up and saw my name sprawled across the front page of the *USA Today* and wondered why I was so average.

People have been taking liberties with my name as long as I can remember my name. It's been GI Joe, Joe-Joe from Komomo, Whatdayaknow, Joe?, Joe blow, Joe schmoe, and even the hideous advertisement of Joe Camel (cough). Now I know how every "Tom, Dick, and Harry" must feel.

They throw my name around as if I am some kind of throw away product, like an Eskimo Pie stick, for instance. Wonder why they don't use Carl..."Carl, Carl from Komomo," or "Whatdayaknow, Horace?" How about referring to every "Arnold Blow" in town got stuck in the snow.

They took an "average" count of the men, I suppose – didn't see anything about a "Josephine average" – just the men – and tallied up the figures regarding male haunts, habits, hobbies, and housing, and "bingo," they think they have us all pegged. Especially if your name is Joe. If you're Amos, well, I'm not sure about your average.

I'm wondering who, where, and how many guys they actually did poll for the results. As usual, nobody called to ask me anything about my haunts and habits. Only the heating duct cleaning man trying to make a sale from cleaning my pipes.

Well, if you, per chance, missed it or forgot about it or didn't care, I'll enlighten you about us males and our "Joe Average" statistics, just so you're in the "Joe know."

At the time of the survey, the "Average Joe" made $29,000 per year, owned one car, watched television about 28 hours a week, ate fast food about three times a week, and engaged in sex – I presumed with the opposite sex – seven times a month. There was more, but this was enough for me to mull on for some time.

The only question I asked my male self was, "Is that really me they studied or some other Joe?" So, I took these five issues and decided to poll myself. From what I hear and read, "$29,000 is barely above the poverty line. I didn't know I was that close. But when I got out my calculator, I found out that what little I seem to make above that figure usually goes to pay the "amount I owe that is more than one-half of the sum on line 56 of the other two parts." Which, if true to form, would surely put me at the poverty line, or your basic "Joe Average" in income.

Next, my eating habits pretty well exclude fast food places, because my doctor told me if I continue to eat bacon-Swiss-guacamole double burgers, with ranch/barbecue sauce on them, I could have a gastric explosion the size of Mount St. Helen. I get served pretty fast at Evan's for Pete's vegetable soup, as well as Stacey's drugs for Juanita's tuna salad, but I don't think that fits me into the "Joe Average" category.

Watching television? Well, it can be addictive, but in my "later state of life," I have learned some disciplines – Kentucky basketball in the winter, Braves in the summer, if they aren't on strike, a movie here and there, and maybe Frazier. I figure the "Joe Averages" of the country watch Rossanne, Married With Children, Tom Parker's Toyota commercials and Vanna White's "big wheel" of fortune. And, if so, and they like that category, please delete "Joe" and stick "Carl" in there.

Automobiles. We have two cars, but actually, my wife owns one, maybe both, if I missed the fine print. I drive both now and then, but mostly the oldest one, because she thinks I'm the oldest. Sounds plausible but it doesn't seem to fit the "Joe Average." Maybe Horace or Sam are average. Let them take the heat.

And then, there's this last category the study mentions. I figure you're wondering. Well, every "Joe" has his limit. That is, every "Joe" has a limit to what he will admit is his limit. And most men will not admit that they are just "average" about this sensitive issue.

So, all I can say is, or all I *will* say in print is, they need to replace my name in their study with Amos, Throckmorton, or Horace. I feel like that old Johnny Cash song. One day I may sing "My name is Sue, how do you do!"

THE BATTLE OF THE SEXES
RAGES IN DECORATED TENTS

God created the universe and rested. Then He created
Man and rested. Then God created woman and since
then, God nor man has been able to rest. (Joke or opinion, take your pick)

I made some predictions early on about what would happen
during the 90s, one of which was that Ross Perot would be
appointed to as Ambassador to Antarctica. Well, predicting is a
dubious process, at best.

Some people made predictions about men and women in the
90s. One ominous overtone related to the "new man" discovering
his inner self. Robert Bly, the poet, writer, and self-proclaimed
guru of a "gathering of men," suggested that communicating at a
deeper level was good for the male spirit, to say nothing of a
healthy digestion.

Growing numbers of men went off for a week-end together,
and, led somewhat loosely by Bly and others, would get in touch
with their feelings which presumably got submerged somewhere
along about the time of the Industrial Revolution.

In addition to discussing maleness, they spent time sitting in
hot tents, sweating, beating tom-toms around a campfire, grunt-
ing and groaning in primeval tones, bringing some catharsis of
the soul.

Accordingly, it helped them rediscover who they are, at least
for a week-end until they get back home and return to the normal
routine of taking out the garbage, changing diapers, and spending
mega-byte hours at the computer, rediscovering again who they
really are. Since there front-page-on-Newsweek beginning, there
have been no grunts to speak of and Robert Bly has disappeared,
and perhaps lives in Antartica with Ross Perot.

Another ominous item given to prediction was about an
eight-year-old girl named Margo from Florida who wanted to
become a member of the Boy Scouts and go on an overnight sum-

mer camp event. Evidently, the Girl Scouts do not tie enough knots, nor do they allow boys, giving some hint to her desire to jump the good G. S. ship lolly-pop.

This was reminiscent of a similar story in the 70s of a girl named Carrie Sue from Houston who had similar desires. I was so struck by her intentions back then that I penned some verse, poetically, which seems appropriate to share here:

"Well, Harvey and Fred and Billy Tate and the scout troop number 268 were having their weekly meeting on a Monday night.

The water safety session had just begun and Harvey played like he had water in his lung, when in walked Carrie Sue, demanding her right.

She said, "I wanna be a girl Boy Scout, tie knots with the boys and go camping out, why, I can swim like fish and cut an X in a rattlesnake bite."

She looked at ole Harvey in his prone situation, said "He needs mouth to mouth Re-susc-i-tation!"

Harvey raised up and yelled, "Let's vote 'er in tonight!"

(Copyright, circa '73)

My further predictions went something like this regarding these two phenomena. The men's so-called "gathering" will fade into oblivion because the women are not going to sit still and let their men start another male organization without them. Ever since Jezebel became a concubine of King Ahab back in B.C. – Before Campouts – the feminine touch has found its way into the male gathering, adding floral curtains with instructions where to hang them, a la, Martha Stewart.

They would creep into the sweaty men's tents and before you can lift a mallet to a tom-tom, they would adjust the temperature to their liking and make the men shave and put on clean underwear. Leadership and program directions would be provided by Oprah, Katy, and Martha. Gatherings of guys would go under covers, er, uh, ground.

When it comes to the Boy/Girl Scout issue, I could see some give and take here. The Boy Scouts of America, of which I was one, I am proud to say (my rank was retired), has gone through many changes. There is still time to do more, still time to respond to the request..."Give us your campfires, your tired rock climbing, your weary knot tier, your merit badge in calf-roping...we'll give you all the cookies you can eat for a month."

I thus predict that one day it may be called the Person Scouts of America.

BEWARE: THERE MAY BE A "GLUT" OF OKRA OUT THERE

In 1994, just when the summertime hit full stride with fresh veggies everywhere for the picking, I read that the vegetable management was "downsizing" okra, the pointy-headed little pods with the prickly hairs.

I made some mention of my distaste for this, well, odious veggie fare in my last book. Many took me to task and others may do the same now. But I can take the heat. Anyway, what was happening back then was that fewer okra pods were proliferating the countryside. Suppliers were dwindling, which meant the supply was dwindling. At least, that's what the okra connoisseurs said.

Suits me fine. Unashamedly, I put okra in a category somewhere between heavy-metal rock music and Jerry Springer – it looks and sounds hideous, and once you taste it, there's not much substance.

In fact, I would go so far as to say an "okra connoisseur" is a full-blown oxymoron. The name itself is foreign to the ear. Sounds like something out of the "Star Wars" movie script. "You Darth Vader, me, Okra." Just doesn't sound edible-friendly.

Gleefully, I called the local agriculture department to get to the meat of the pod, as it were, and see if I could begin celebrating the demise of the dreaded "O" in earnest. I received some interesting information, but when I indicated my distaste for the stuff, the okra-information person accused me of not being from the south.

Well, technically, that is true, being from western Kentucky. But southwest Kentucky is close enough to okra for me. My mother loved it, along with cooked turnips and stewed tomatoes – vegetables that children's nightmares are made of. Thankfully, I wasn't okra-abused as a wee child.

Then the agri-person explained some background and noted that veggie historians believe okra originated in Ethiopia. That's in Africa, south of Egypt, and some distance away from where the Garden of Eden is supposed to have been. This confirms my theory that there was no okra on the farm of Adam and Eve. I hate to disappoint you okra lovers, especially the Baptist brethren and sistren, who, by the way, find ingenious methods of slipping okra parts in most every casserole they bring to church events.

My okra-source continued to say that "they think it came to America on ships through the port of New Orleans." I figured it was promptly sliced up and added to the jambalaya pot, giving the late Hank Williams added sustenance for his immortal "Goodbye Joe" song about "a crawfish pie and a filè gumgo."

The okra pod spokesperson concluded with a "kicker" of information, saying that there really was no shortage of okra, but rather, a "glut" in the market and that production was decreasing for the time being. This did not sound good to me. Here we had an "okra glut," which I figured was what you got in your throat if you're unlucky enough to swallow a very large amount.

What this meant was that the okra people, ever vigilant to popularize their produce, would find a way to pawn off the surplus on the innocent, unsuspecting public in some exotic dinner fare. One day I might find okra hairs deep down in my tossed salad, hiding under some cucumber or carrot part.

Why, the new "fat conscious" school diet police might try to change the lunchroom menu with a new item called "the Green Slug." Just the mention of the "O" word sends chills down the spines of children. No school dietition in his or her right mind would place okra on the menu and live to tell about it.

Frankly, I don't believe God created okra. I rather think it was manufactured somewhere south of the Nile River and brought up by the Queen of Sheba and served to Solomon as a plot to make his many wives and concubines jealous. I believe further that he was unimpressed. In fact, he began the 17th chapter of Proverbs with the words, "Better is a dry morsel, and quietness therewith, (say, a fig) than an hour full of sacrifices (insert okra) with strife."

Okay, so it's a liberal interpretation, but I'm still staying okra-free.

IF STATE LEGISLATURE DECREES ENGLISH THE NATIVE LANGUAGE, WHERE DOES "GEORGIAN" FIT IN, Y'ALL?

Around the mid-nineties, the state legislators discussed making English the official language of our fair state. Indubitably! I thought English was already official, though I find it more and more difficult to understand various southern accents these days.

Why just the other day, I asked a fellow shopper at the grocery store if he happened to know where the bouillon cubes section might be. "Vcew, joshc shockg al dosnen, donkashay," he answered, pointing to the shelf right in front of me.

"Well, bless Pat," I retorted, noticing a jar of cubes sitting there under my dosnen. "Donkashay right back at ya." I wasn't sure of his native country, thinking at first he may be on a preliminary visit for the Olympics. But on second look, I determined by the Georgia Tech cap that he was probably an exchange student from lower Alabama.

As a native from another state, there were those who considered my "tongue" to be foreign when I first came to reside here. However, as one serving in the ministry, you can understand that I have practiced religiously, you might say, on speaking "Georgian" with the best of them, y'all.

Frankly, I just needed to "get with the program." Southern writers seem to write in Georgian in most every book I have read. You remember dear Scarlet flippantly dressing down the young men at Twelve Oaks, "Wah-uh, wah-uh, wah-uh...fiddle-dee-dee, that's all you baw-ys tawk about, anyway."

Of course, public figures such as the late senator "Hummun" Talmadge and President Jimmy "Caahtuh" always spoke Georgian when they addressed their people. In fact, we could almost have three official languages if you consider North Georgian mountain twang, South Georgian drawl for those below the gnat-line, and Atlanta Georgian for those who have "citified" their accent.

I asked friend, Jeff, the high school physics teacher, how he looked at the official language possibility. "On the one hand, you feel you should help all students, regardless of dialectical background. On the other hand, if English is our official language, we should help all students to be proficient, effective citizens." The guy ought to be a politician!

He gave me an example of how that might work. He once had a French student who spoke little English. Another student who took good notes, gave them to the school's French teacher, whose class translated the notes into French, helping the aforementioned French student to keep up in Jeff's physics class.

Sounded like a good idea, but I would ask which is the official language here – French, English, or physics? I took French once and "bonjour, petitie-pie" was about the extent of my mastery.

I decided to discuss this English language proposed legislation with another expert, lawyer W. Johnson, the dapperly, suspended litigator who labors deep in the bowels of Atlanta's concrete jungle. "Small potatoes in Georgia," he said. "Bigger issue in Texas and California where they stir a bigger pot and have a language all their own."

"What about an official national language?" I asked. "Was English ever made into a law here in years past?"

"Don't think it was ever official. Came over with the British, of course. Perhaps we decided to bloody take it for granted, so to speak."

"Poor Indians," I said, "guess they didn't have a vote on the subject."

"Yeah, it was all Creek to them...or was it Iroquois?" he asked, slyly. W. J. is quick on his feet in a courtroom.

So, if English is made Georgia's official language in the near future, I recommend that an addendum be attached. Because one night I heard a TV reporter interviewing a young high school lass in north Georgia about the road conditions that caused schools to close up there, and she said, "Weather warn't that bad. We could've went, anyway."

So, the real question is, if English is voted in as an official language, does it come with an order of grammar on the side?

PART II

**THE APRIL FOOL'S 15TH…THE TADPOLE TAX,
TALKING AMONG THE TALKING HEADS,
AND OTHER SUCH "DOODLY-SQUAT"**

APRIL 15 –
THE NEW "APRIL FOOL'S DAY"

"The only difference between death and taxes is that
death doesn't get worse every time the congress meets"
Will Rogers

A man went to see the funeral director and asked to be cremated and have his ashes put in a box addressed to the federal government with a note which said, "Now you have it all!"

And under the category of "some things never change," in 1991, the Senate took one of their more bodacious votes, "taxing" on a raise to the new year's budget. Ostensibly, it was one of those "one-ups-manship" moves on the House members, who were making more money than some in the Senate – at last count. They didn't want Newt the Grinch to get ahead of the "senior members."

I believe it was the "Honora-bull" Robert Byrd who said, "It would bee-hoove us to receive such a raise, so that we could provide better service for the American people." Honest folks, that's almost a direct pile of, uh, er, quote.

We shouldn't begrudge the senators from having a raise now and then, with inflation, the cost of paper shredders, and all. I'd certainly agree to, say, a dollar a month – before taxes. That would get them an extra Twinkie, as if they don't have enough "twinkies" as it is. But as you may remember, this wasn't any 59 cent snack out of our pocket, this was second mortgage size raise per senator - $23,000. Enough Twinkies to cover Montana, huh?

They voted on this late in the night after the press and certain other innocent bystanders went home. After hours, they deliberated on the wage-salary raise just because the house members "make more than we do." They said they would trade off the speaking fees received from special interest groups who help keep them in office, and instead, they'll take this raise as remuneration. What a bunch of guys!

So, they voted themselves a raise and promised to give us better service while "taxing" on some extra for you and me to pay, along with a poor guy named J. C. Hyde, an 82-year-old farmer who still works some of his 125-acre, third generation farm outside of Atlanta. Now he finds that the IRS wants almost half a million in taxes for it, just because "he's not plowing it all for crops," and therefore, it doesn't qualify as an active farm. One can only sympathize with him and his plight with the government.

And so, like Snoopie with helmet, goggles, and scarf atop his doghouse, muttering "Here's the Great Red Baron..." – it is April and we citizens sit with calculator, sharpened pencils, and receipts of a traveling kind, muttering to ourselves, "Here's the great April Fool in his "tax-plane"...flying it for another year.

I try desperately to decide if the greater portion on line 53 is subtracted from or more than or susceptible to placing in a "blind" trust for a seeing-eye tax accountant to make sense out of what I should multiply by what is left over...on line 58.

I suppose most of us wonder why we can't simplify this system...the old "keep it simple, stupid" way. I have come to believe that the IRS wants to make it complicated so they can hide more tax costs and thus, *"keep us simply stupid."* Why can't we play the old percentage thing, one category, one check. You make so much, you pay so much.

My friend and former IRS worker, Mr. I. Ben Dunning, said, "We don't care what the rules are, we just collect." He explained that there are too many agencies, bureaus, and that we have a large deduction system, i.e. mortgages, church, interest, twinkies, etc. It is a snowballing thing.

On a TV "talk taxes" show, a tax expert said they want to be more "user friendly." Ha, I thought. They are attempting to lure those who have never filed to "come out and know we'll be happy to work with you." Like the line by Robert De Niro in the thriller movie "Cape Fear"..."come out, come out, wherever you are." That's scary.

Tell you something else that's scary. On the same TV show, the expert said the IRS is giving a reward of 10% of whatever the person owes to the person who turns him or her in. Pull your shades, boys, and dim the lights - Big Brother is watching to see if the amount on line 43 is any bigger than last year. I didn't make this up!

25

SPEAKING OF BIG BROTHER, TADPOLE TAX IN AIR SPACE?

The federal government levies enough taxes for various and sundry projects to cause all concerned citizens to mutter, "I'll be a suck-egg mule!" In fact, congress might pass legislation to study why a mule would want to suck an egg in the first place. But they're already researching why the chicken crossed the road, deducing that their vote indicated the chicken-study comes before the egg-study.

Anyway, another place our taxes went during the 90s was right into thin air...space air. The space shuttle, Endeavour, blasted off one week-end, bobbing around the planet at some astronomically, astronautical speed, while its inhabitants did whatever they do while bobbing.

I always thought their job had something to do with satellite handoffs and hook-ups, taking pictures of stars and galaxies for future routes through the black hole, firing rocket boosters to get them back home and reporting to Houston space center of the possible sightings of Darth Vader, leader of the Evil Empire.

I found out that we have a misconception of how our tax dollars work in space. For one thing, NASA relaxed its ruling that no married couple can "astronaut" together on the same shuttle. So, on this particular trip, they allowed the first "space-couple" to go and do something, we're not sure exactly what.

But according to the report, a "study" was to take place in the kitchen by one of the astronauts. I can't imagine anything in a shuttle vaguely resembling a kitchen. But this trip, they studied how bread yeast would rise, if, in fact, it does rise at all. I wondered if the "Mrs. Astronaut" tended to the bread, but they never told us.

I also wondered if there was some subtle message to this endeavor in Endeavour. Was there something about family values on board? Was President Bush I in on making the first astronaut couple rise to the occasion, and have Mrs. Astronaut be the first to bake chocolate chip cookies on his watch?

26

Does family values communicate well if they both help with the cookies, realizing that you just can't up and go for a walk if you get upset with each other. I mean, it's dark out there. Perhaps the study implies that baking chocolate chip cookies prevents "divorce in space," a possible future sitcom. We never got a report of a break-up.

But there was more. Tax money helped with further studies...on the 7600 fruit flies, the two Japanese carp, and 30 chicken eggs. (I ain't making this up either folks). But rather than comment on that, I would ask about the four female South African clawed frogs which, as I understand, were observed endeavoring to ovulate in the Endeavour, rendering our astronauts with valuable information as to the life of a tadpole in space.

No, you didn't read that wrong...I said female frogs ovulating. I mean, if they can talk about giving condoms to teenagers in high school, then we can talk here about female South African clawed frogs ovulating in space. I'm not sure if "Froggy went a-courtin'" was background music or not. But my only question is, "Why?" To my knowledge, there's no answer.

I can imagine Kermit the Frog was elated to know some of his species were on the space ride of their life. But if Miss Piggy gets wind of it, we might be spending tax dollars on the rooting habits of piglets in space. Oink!

BIG TOE PREVENTS CELEBRATION OF VETERAN'S DAY

A retired general raised white leghorn chickens. A big white rooster strutted around in the hen house. One day the general decided to breed the chickens with a big red rooster which he put in the hen house with the other rooster. The very next morning, he heard an awful commotion and peered in the hen house. The red rooster was lying on the floor, beaten to a pulp and the rest of the white leghorn hens were in a long row, beak to beak. The first rooster strutted down the line and shouted, "Now ladies, when I say that the uniform of the day is white, I do mean white!"

When the Gulf War came to an end in the early 90s, General Norman Schwarzkopf retired from leading "warz" efforts around the world. Word had it that he wanted to spend his time going about the countryside making speeches, live on the coast of South Carolina and write a book about his war exploits and all that was attached thereto at the time. You could bet your combat boots that he would make a tidy sum from such endeavors.

Talk show hosts asked him about politics, to which the general responded "No way" rather emphatically. You can't help but love this man, who faintly resembles a tough, but rather cherubic Jonathan Winters. But if he had become a politician, it's a good possibility his countenance would have turned from cherubic to pock-marked, maybe over night. People wanted him to lead just about every parade and with our country's newly found patriotism at the time, he was a natural.

However, all the euphoria of those days conjured up by our Gulf War involvement caused me some "war memories" difficulty. Actually, embarrassment is more like it. You see, the good general and I are about the same age and we came up during the same era, those "good ole" World War II days in the 40s. We were kids, and people of that generation merely spoke of it as *"The"* war.

Under normal circumstances, I might have had the opportunity to wear the Army green or the "chocolate chip" camouflage uniforms of today and become a great warrior myself. But as fate and one big toe would have it, I never got to go down the "war path" of fighting history.

I know...you're wondering what is it about the big toe. Well, it is a long family story. You know, "my grandfather was an old Indian fighter. He married an old Indian." It gets worse from there, so I'll condense it. I actually joined an Army reserve unit in Kentucky after I left college and was sent to Fort Knox, the great gold center, where some years later, James Bond fought Goldfinger and won, as usual.

It was a special services unit designed for recreation purposes through which I would be able to play basketball and ping pong close to the PX and serve my six months of active duty, followed by six years of reserves. (I'm not making this up!)

During the first three weeks of basic training, I learned to make the blanket on my bed so tight I could bounce a ping pong ball on it. Forest Gump would have been proud. I also learned to get up at 4:30 in the morning, an absolutely ungodly experience. Up to then, I didn't think there was a 4:30 a.m.

One day, we were marched to the base hospital for physical exams, where we had to take shots, give our medical history, and turn our heads to cough. It was there that a lieutenant doctor saw my big toe, which was pointing in a northeasterly direction, looked at it and exclaimed, (I'm not making this up, either) "We can't use toes like that. The best thing for you to do is go home." I gladly accepted my fateful diagnosis and kissed the silver bar on his shoulder.

Returning to the barracks, my platoon sergeant, Sgt. Esubio Gonzales (real name), whom I had previously judged was a direct descendent of Pancho Villa, was more succinct about the matter. "Carrumba!" he shouted with expletives, which meant in "Pancho-ese," that I was a lilly-livered, "gold brick," lower-than-a-private person.

He assigned me to the barracks for the rest of my stay and the next five weeks, I was Permanent Barracks Orderly, or the ranking PBO of the latrine. Then, I was out, skedaddle, scram, F-9, or some such classification I don't know the meaning of even to this day. And, I'm not even classified as a veteran. All that latrine work, down the drain, so to speak.

So now, our country has become more and more patriotic over the 90s and when the local bands and orchestras play the Armed Service songs, I'm left out. You know how it goes..."When we get to your branch's song, stand and be counted while we sing,"...I don't get to stand and be applauded. It would be nice if they played the "Big Toe Blues," but I guess that will never happen.

I envy the old General Norman with his "war-cuddly" mannerisms. He's popular, leader of the parade and probably rich by now. I'll bet he has a handsome big toe inside his combat boot, too.

TALK MAY BE CHEAP, BUT THERE'S PLENTY OF IT IN WASHINGTON

"The less you say, the less you have to take back."
High school basketball coach
(May not be original, but I heard it first from him)

I'm not sure where the expression, "talk's cheap," came from, but it didn't come from Washington. Up there, it's an expensive proposition. Maybe that's what Eve said to the serpent when it spouted off about the tree of knowledge. "Talk's cheap" may have gotten her in trouble. Didn't turn out too well, I'm sorry to say.

Anyway, there does seem to be a lot of "cheap" talking these days. There's lots of phone talk, for example. You can always hang up, but most of us listen patiently. However, some people – we all know them – have a penchant for "yip-yapping," as my dear sister-in-law used to say. One morning, I was sitting at local eatery, Evan's Fine Foods, with my coffee and paper. A woman sat down at the booth across the aisle.

Soon, a man joined her with a "How ya doin'?" and then proceeded into conversational infinity with something about religion and certain other minutia which I tried desperately to tune out as I read (didn't read!) my paper. I believe the woman was able to connect two, maybe three sentences during his blathering "cheap talk."

Believe it or not, that same evening, my wife, sister-in-law and I were dining out and two couples came in and sat at the next booth. As it turned out, I was facing the man of one couple who was talking as he slid into his seat and began giving "talk's cheap" new meaning.

For the duration of our meal – some 45 minutes – he went on and on about some kind of business deal he was working on with virtually no conversation whatsoever from the other three people. I'm not making this up...for almost 10 minutes, he "yip-yapped" with not so much as a "really" from any other person. Unbelieveable!

Admittedly, I have always thought women could outdo men in the "talk-the-horns-off-a-billy-goat" department. But, believe me, men are close behind if not forging ahead. Who among us doesn't run for cover when we see the "talker" coming, letting us know the latest information about his golf match yesterday, the new SUV, or "did I tell you about my operation last month?"

Well, as I have stated from the outset of this little piece, the talk in Washington is not cheap, and it's no different, and it is constant. One night shortly after the congressional elections, I was watching the news program now called the News Hour with Jim Lehrer. Mr. Lehrer was questioning five "freshmen" congresspersons (a more appropriate descriptive adjective could not be found).

There were three Republicans, two Democrats, one Jewish, one African-American, one gray headed, one redheaded, one slightly balding, three women, two men. States represented were California, Utah, Indiana, Pennsylvania and one I forgot. Must have been Texas. Fits, huh? We're talking (and talking) politically correct here.

This program has a sophisticated format, though it started off with a mundane question. "Well, now that you're in Washington and on the federal payroll, what do you think.?" Mr. Lehrer asked. Not his exact words, but close enough.

Off they went, yip-yapping about "appreciation for my opposing colleague" and "I'll tell you, this is really fun." They talked of issues "the American people want," and what "my constituency sent me here to do." Does anyone believe anything these people say, I wanted to ask?

Personally, I had never laid eyes on any one of the five and I would doubt that few of their constituency had said much to them about "what they want," but boy, were they talking it up. And the most significant thing was the manner in which each "side" seemed to present facts with their own style of "gobbledygook," while the other side peered disapprovingly across the table.

When the Republican was talking, the Democrat was shaking his or her head.

When the Democrat was talking, the Republican was shaking his or her head. Talking Heads, followed by shaking heads. The great question for us "un-congress" persons is who talks and who shakes the most credibly, if in fact, a Washington head can talk or shake credibly at all?

The politicians up there must think the American people are imbeciles. Given the way they talk, as well as shake their heads, and the way we vote to send them back or vote one out and send yet another to continue talking and shaking, I suppose they are right. And in the context of this subject, perhaps I have said too much about it anyway.

Like my coach said, "the less you say, the less you have to take back." But I am hard-pressed to take back anything I said here. So, maybe "talk's cheap." But, then, so's this book.

NIGHTMARE OF FIFTH GRADE ARITHMETIC IS REOCURRING

Teacher: If I take a potato, cut it in halves, then in quarters, then cut each piece in half, what will I have?
Pupil: Potato Salad.

It was the worst nightmare of every 11-year-old in Miss Martha Henry Gregory's fifth grade class back in western Kentucky. She would amble up the aisle behind me while I labored feverishly over one of her famous arithmetic tests. She would pause at my desk-side, peering over my shoulder to see how I was doing, as I hunkered down over my paper – pencil in one hand, counting fingers on the other.

I knew I didn't know beans about how to figure out the answers. And she knew I didn't know beans about how to figure out the answer. And the nightmare was knowing she might call on me to give the answer out loud after the test and expose my lousy finger-counting dexterity.

If Johnny had 17 apples, and he gave four to his classmates who didn't have any and he lost two more because they rotted in the bag, what percentage of the total number of apples would be left after he presented the required quota to the apple-to-the-teacher fund? I could add fine, as long as I could look at my fingers. I could subtract if I was allowed to "carry" what I was subtracting to the next column. But percentages, fractions, and pie-are-squares were an abomination to me, and the Lord, too, probably.

Imagine, for example, the trouble Noah must have had trying to understand the discussion of dimensions for the ark, with fifty cubits here and thirty cubits there. It's almost as difficult, I would think, as understanding the government's budget process, to say nothing of what their "process" totals. Which leads me to this.

Every year, the president and his accountants send the congress a budget and in some generalized fashion, it "trickles down" to us regular folks and we try to make sense of it. Let's see, if we have 42 billion barrels of apples, and we send 2 billion barrels to Israel and 13 billion to Brazil, how many will be left to fill an ark 24 cubits by 18 cubits which will be sailing up the river to, say, Des Moines, Iowa for canning during the rainy season?

I'm sitting here slumped over the kitchen table trying to figure what percentage of my tax money goes here and what goes there. I know I don't know and they know in Washington that I don't know, regardless of how much counting I do on my fingers. One president said we could "read his lips," while years later, his son talked about "fuzzy math."

And back in the 90s there was "Bill Clintax," which hardly no one understood. He came out with some kind of paper listing over 200 items described as "winners and losers," indicating what would be spent and what would be cut. Here's what I read in the paper…To spend on energy…"Renewable energy and conservation programs: Add $1.3 billion." (which we will pay taxes for, of course)

To cut on subsidies – "Electric power: Collect 1.7 billion by raising prices on electricity generated by 123 federal dams." (which we will pay in utility increases). Go figure them apples.

Then later, I saw an interview on TV with a domino player in Texas. He was talking about energy and said, (I'm not making this up), "He's (the president) up there talking about BTUs, and I bet half the country don't know what a BTU is in the first place." Well, I'll admit it would be a bit tough for the average citizen.

But it did remind me of a story that seems apropos for the moment…of an old farmer who wandered into the local town hardware store and said he wanted to purchase a new hot water heater for his wife.

The clerk asked, "How many B-T-Us ya need?"

"Well," the farmer answered, scratching his head, "I need enough B-T-Us to heat a B-U-T as big as a T-U-B." Which may or may not have anything to do with our government arithmetic lesson, but I think I'm in the same fix I was in the fifth grade.

If memory serves me right, I didn't do too well on the test and probably should have written a note at the bottom of the page and told the teacher to take all the apples and distribute them as she sees fit. In essence, I think that's what congress does with our taxes, anyway.

U.S. POST OFFICE-APPROVED COW GRAZING SAVES MONEY

The new preacher's first sermon was on Wednesday evening. The only person who showed up was an old farmer. The preacher decided to preach his sermon anyway, lasting over an hour. Afterward, he asked the farmer what he thought of his sermon and the farmer replied, "Well, okay, I guess, but I'll tell ya, when I take a load of hay to feed my cows and only one shows up, I sure don't feed 'er the whole load."

You probably missed the story some years back that came out of Louisville, Kentucky about cows being used to save money for a local post office on the outskirts of the city. Don't lose me here. The manager of the post office decided to "hire" some cows – about eight or so – and let them feast on a couple of government-owned acres right next to the post office buildings.

Ostensibly, this would save on the cost of maintaining said acreage. Dandelions and other assorted weeds would become fodder for the cows. In return the gracious cows would provide bovine lawn care at its best...fertilizing the lawn frequently, as well as munching it to a reasonably manicured, lower level.

I thought this was a bodacious plan and I applaud the post office industry of Louisville. For one thing it would save money, which I will address momentarily. But more than that, it would bring some much needed prominence to the poor cow, which has fallen on hard times over recent years because of vegetarians and assorted health purists.

You've heard all the "reports" about fatty content from contented cows, tainted beef stories, Oprah beef suits, Wendy's bacon-flavored, cheddar cheeseburgers, and the wonderful but "contaminated with fat substance" chocolate milk. Then there's "mad-cow" disease which comes, I presume, from discontented cows and cold milking machines.

Although I did not grow up on a farm, I spent many hours of quality time visiting two different family farms as a lad. Both of my grandfathers had a farm. I had some experience with cows during those years. You might say, "Joe knows cows." My grandfathers would not say that, but I would.

I never had a cow for a pet, but I did try to pet one once when I was about 6 years old. My mistake was attempting to pet it while my grandfather was milking the sucker. He – or she, couldn't figure which – lodged one of its hind size 12 hooves right in my little tummy. Pretty well turned me against the idea of milking – a ghastly job of trying to get milk by pulling hard on one of four things down around the cow's "private parts."

One thing I know about cows is how much they like to chew. They can chew on their "cud" for hours. They swallow that wad and next thing you know, up it comes and they start chewing it again. It seems like the more they swallow, the more they chew, sorta like the congress. They can chew on something and vote to swallow it, then, the next thing you know they regurgitate it up and start chewing on it again.

What really struck me about this post office manager's great idea was the amount of money that can be saved by letting cows do something useful during a time when cow products are in a recession because of health-conscious persons. I read where a Jersey cow, for example, produces the most butterfat of any milk cow in all of cowdom. Rather than producing so many fat grams, retrain some of them vocationally, and let them "munchmow" lawns.

The post office manager in Louisville thought he could save some $4000 in maintenance fees of the government property in one year. Multiply that by the savings on yard maintenance of umpteen post office yards, governor's mansions, the Washington mall and even the White house, and you have a substantial savings. Of course, congress would set up a cow maintenance bureaucracy involving thousands of people at thousands of dollars and result in more chewing and swallowing.

I know this is not going to happen. And you know this is not going to happen. We love our chocolate milk and we love our hamburgers, cows or no cows. And the poor manager of that post office had a good idea, but by now is probably raising tobacco, a staple of disdain in Kentucky, beside the post office.

And I can say with good authority that that is a different kind of "cud" to chew which you had better not swallow, even once!

CONGRESSWOMAN SAYS COLLEAGUE DOESN'T KNOW "SQUAT!"

Well, actually she added more to it, but let me explain. I was watching C-Span on TV one night sometime back in the middle of "the nines." There was a motion on the floor of the House to cut aid to poor little Haiti and a dear Florida congresswoman in a hat was speaking passionately against the motion and saying, as congresspersons often do, how the American government should care for such countries – financially, politically, socially, recreationally, spiritually, now and forever, a-men – along with other political mumbo-jumbo which congresspersons speak.

Now most of us know more about pulpwood drivers in south Georgia than we do about what's going on in Haiti. But I sat straight up in my sloucher-chair when the dear congresswoman's voice began to crack.

She forthrightly admonished her colleague from Florida who had moved to cut the aid, by saying, among other things, "You sir, don't know doodly-squat about the people of Haiti."

As I often do when watching certain congresspersons on TV, I shouted at the lady from my chair…"Doodly-squat? Did you say doodly-squat?" laughing at this verbal assault. She continued, even though the House speaker banged his gavel, indicating time was about up for her. She begged for just another minute and he was touched.

She became more emotional during further imploring and, looking at her opponent, she said once again that he didn't know "doodly-squat about Haiti!"

I about fell out of my sloucher-chair and hollered again, "you tell 'em lady, they don't know doodly-squat about Haiti and a lot of other things besides." I became passionate myself, as I gave my own "citizen's piece of mind" on the issue.

"Gore doesn't know doodly-squat about e-mail.

"Hillary doesn't know doodly-squat about my health needs.

"Gingrich doesn't know doodly-squat about the farmers.

"Dan Quayle doesn't know doodly-squat about doodly-squat."

These were just a few examples of my passion. I am sure other citizens can think of people in their circle, as well as other politicians who don't know doodly-squat about whatever it is they think they do. In fact, this is one of the premier expressions in all the land regarding what people know and don't know. And now it was being used in the halls of congress by a congresswoman in a hat.

I decided to look this one up in the dictionary, thinking, as I thumbed through the pages, that it was probably just another phrase attributed to some indiscriminate hill woman of the late 1800s, expressing to her husband what he basically didn't know about raising hogs in West Virginia.

But lo, there it was in the latest edition of Webster. Boy, did I get a jolt! It said, "n. doo-dle-Y-squat; euphemism for s____." I think you get the picture here. I also looked up the word, euphemism. It said, "The substitution of an inoffensive expression for one that may suggest something unpleasant."

What the Florida congresswoman in the hat did on the floor of the House, it seemed to me, was to speak her piece about the Haiti issue without being offensive to her colleague, while telling him at the same time that what he really knew about the issue he had so eloquently brought to the floor was as unpleasant as, well, "doodly-squat."

As Ross Perot might say, "I find that fascinatin', don't you?"

PART III

JULY, 1996A.D.—IN THE YEAR OF OUR OLYMPICS

JULY, 1996A.D.—
IN THE YEAR OF OUR OLYMPICS

Right in the middle of the "Last Of The Nines," there came a world-wide event that pretty well captured Georgia's capitol city...the Summer Olympics. Until 1996, over the past millennium, it had been held in the United States only twice - in Los Angeles both times. This time was different – very different

When it was announced years earlier, it was announced merely as "Atlanta." It seemed difficult to say Atlanta, Georgia. "Atlanta" seemed exotic, new age, a city straining out of the depths toward golden towers. To the "natives," however, it was just the capitol of our state, where the likes of Herman, Jimmy, and Zell held "state court," where Valdastans drive up to for a Braves' game once a year, or drive through on their way to the Smokeys.

But in the summer of '96, we were on the map of the world for all to see...Mohammed Ali shakily lighting the torch, Richard Jewel being dogged as a suspect in a bombing of Centennial Park, and Billy Payne putting on the face of something other than a Georgia good-ole-boy. Turned out pretty well. But I doubt it will be back for oh, say another millennium.

Here's my experience.

OLYMPIC VOLUNTEER JOB NOT QUITE SO GLAMOROUS

It was about the biggest event to hit Atlanta since Rhett and Scarlett showed up at the Grand theater on December 15, 1939 for the premiere of "Gone With The Wind." The 1996 Olympic Games – summertime version – was about to start and at the time, I didn't have any specific assignment. Let me explain before you laugh.

In April 1995, I read an advertisement in the paper giving instructions to high-tail it over to the Decatur Library to fill out official forms if I wanted to be a volunteer for the '96 Olympics. I high-tailed it and was given a booklet of forms, asking questions about my status in life - address, social security number, debts, quirks, past employment, was I married, did I drive, and had I ever been in jail in Sinking Fork, Kentucky. There is a Singing Fork, Kentucky, but they don't have a jail. So I was clean.

I dutifully completed the forms and mailed them to the ACOG office. To be honest, I didn't believe I would get an assignment, thinking of the great hordes of Atlantans who also wanted to volunteer, get a keepsake uniform, and get to kiss the ring of Billy Payne, ACOG chief and Knight of Georgia.

But I figured if I wanted to work in a special place, this was my chance to ask for it. So, I asked for an assignment at the Olympic Stadium down on the field, inside the oval track, handing out medals to winning athletes, as they bowed before me on the platform. My second choice was to drive the basketball "Dream Team" to McDonalds for hamburger breaks. As you would imagine, I didn't get either one.

However, fate smiled on me, albeit somewhat wryly, and I received a telephone call in March of '96 telling me that I had, in fact, been "chosen," I believe is how the person phrased it. "Your venue location," the official noted, "is the Olympic Stadium." I 'bout had a holy spasm right there on the phone.

He went on to say that I would be working with "security." When I heard that word, the hairs on the back of my neck stood up. I might, he went on, have an assignment at the "venue VIP access point" or down on the field "assisting athletes." My neck hairs began to lie down and relax, calmly. The assignment sounded like something that could be "a chance in a lifetime," a phrase that everyone in the sound of the mayor's voice heard over and over prior to this big event.

When I hung up the phone, I happily told my dear wife, Virginia, that I had been selected to work at the Olympic Stadium. "Doing what?" she asked with a raised eyebrow.

"Security," I answered, confidently.

"Well, I am sure the visitors from outer Mongolia will be in good hands," she chortled, amused, I'm sure, at the thought of my keeping the delegation of 250 Mongols safe while crossing Hank Aaron Drive to board the bus back to the dorm at Georgia Tech.

During the next few weeks, I received a manual and video which told how to search bags with a smile, how to point in various languages toward the bathrooms (which is pretty universal...the pointing, not the bathrooms), and how to handle an argument between a visitor from Spain and a visitor from Italy over the referee's ruling during their team's soccer match. (Think Tech fan vs Georgia fan.)

About a month before the Games, I attended my first training session with other "volunteer security persons" as yet unaware of location and job. We listened as those in charge instructed us about handling people who lost their tickets or their babies, and what to do with the guy named Bubba who thinks the event at the stadium is a pre-season game for the Falcons. I began to wonder about the wisdom of even filling out forms in the first place.

Then, about two weeks before the opening day, I went to pick up my uniform. I received a badge with my picture which was made earlier, my white shirt with a "security" patch on it, my hideous-shade-of-green pants, black tennis shoes like retired preachers wear, a plastic water bottle I could strap around my waist, and my pith helmet. That's right, a pith helmet. I didn't know what it was, either.

Remember the old Tarzan movies, and the crook, a white guy with a thin mustache, who shouted at the natives to carry all the boxes? You remember the helmet he wore? That's a pith helmet. It's an ugly sort of chapeau if there ever was one, but as the people told us, "it'll be a collector's item." (No one has touched it at any of my latest garage sales!)

Just a few days prior to the celebrated opening ceremonies, we were all asked to come to the Olympic stadium for "on site training." The first place I needed to go when arriving was the men's room. For some reason, I got locked in. Not for long, but long enough to make me think how lowly this assignment was. But I did feel secure…in the restroom.

I learned to point to this room in many languages!

MY BRIEF MOMENT OF FAME, HOLDING THE OLYMPIC FLAME

(Well, actually the flame was out)

The great torch was handed to me. I held it in my right hand like all the other "bearers" held it while making their torch-carrying trek from Athens (and that ain't Georgia) to Atlanta for the Olympic Games.

It wasn't lit, I'm sorry to say, and I didn't go running down the street through cheering crowds in loose fitting shorts and frumpy tennis shoes, holding it high and lifted up. It would have been a signal honor to be asked, but, lo, it wasn't to be. But I got to hold it for a few seconds.

Of course, it was one of many, but probably the first one off the assembly line. The person who let me hold it is Sharon Shelton, who was director of the Office of Uniform Distribution for volunteers working during the Olympics. She was the one responsible for presenting me with my trusty pith helmet, the dear child.

The reason she had it was because her husband, Sam, was project manager of a six-member team from Georgia Tech which had the responsibility of designing the '96 torch. She brought it to a meeting where she was speaking.

Sam and Sharon have been friends since back in the 60s. Before this job, Sharon was Director of Volunteer Services for many years at what was then Georgia Baptist Hospital of Atlanta. Sam has taught off and on for years at Tech in mechanical engineering, but is really an ingenious inventor and entrepreneur by trade.

There's also some personal background here. Sam's grandparents were from my hometown in Kentucky and also members of the church where I "grew up in Jesus name." I'll tell you only this much...One night in my younger, more "stupider" days, Sam's grandfather saved my rear-end with his tractor by pulling my car (er, Dad's car) out of a ditch on a country road near his farm. And, to quote Forrest Gump, "that's all I have to say about tha-yet!"

I have been eternally grateful to Mr. Shelton for that act of mercy and when I found out years later of that family connection, I immediately concluded, "Any grandson of Mr. Shelton's is a friend of mine!" I have never had to call Sam and ask to be pulled out of any ditch in Atlanta, but if I were ever stuck in some "desperate" spot, I believe he would find a tractor and be there.

Anyway, as you might know, I was dazzled by the opportunity to see and "carry" the torch, even for a minute in the hallway, knowing the family connection with this torch and its lead creator. And the creation wasn't easy.

It had to weigh only four pounds, burn for at least 30 minutes in rain, sleet, or snow, and have a design commensurate with the Greek history of the games, as well as uniqueness to this Olympic's Centennial year. Here's what they came up with.

It was 32 inches high, tallest ever for the summer games and designed to resemble 22 reeds, one for each of the modern Olympic games. The handle was Georgia pecan wood. The gold band above the handle featured the Atlanta 1996 logo and quilt of leaves motif, and the name of each host city for the past century etched on the gold band near the base of the torch.

Some 10,000 were made for the many runners who had the opportunity of a lifetime to carry the flaming torch, as they handed it off, one to another. And, of course, it had to be designed not to go out during the 30 or so minute relay by each carrier, which in Sam's mind was probably a "piece of cake," though he didn't let on.

So the torch was lit with the proper pomp and ceremony in Athens, Greece, and soon "flown" to Los Angeles for its 84-day trip to Atlanta. I was generally impressed with the "carriers" of the torch and, in addition to television reports, watched it being carried down the street right in front of my church. There were athletes like Rafer Johnson, former decathlon Gold medal winner, and handicapped persons like Kourtney Swanson, valiantly carrying it high while walking with her crutch.

47

There were a lot of other dignitaries who had their 30 minutes of fame-with-the-flame, some of who were "big wheels" and some not so big. However, even though I watch their show now and then, I thought Pat and Vanna were a little our of character, though I suppose they could be called "big wheels of good fortune" to be able to carry it their allotted time.

No one invited me to be a big wheel, so my claim to torch fame was that I got to hold it and I know the creator, as well as his wonderful grandfather. I bet he could win a medal in the "tractor pull."

(Personal note: Our dear friend, Sharon Shelton, died of cancer in the spring of 2003 She left a wonderful legacy for her daughters, Stacy and Suzie, and husband, Sam.)

OPENING NIGHT...
PROTECTING THE PRESIDENT, THE DANCING BUTTERFLIES, AND THE PERUVIAN PRESS

(Or, where is the bullet from
Barney Fife's pocket when I need it)

It was the afternoon before the evening's Opening Ceremonies. After sitting in the "briefing room" for about an hour, waiting for our final training, the "commander" announced to the 500 or so volunteer security personnel present, "We have received word that our Special Training supervisors are stuck in traffic along the Olympic torch route. So, (looking up into the crowd), John, you come down and take 25 people, and Ellis, you come and take another 25,...etc.

After about another hour, I got to leave with 25 others, following Robert whoever, as he led us to our place of service to "secure" the stadium for President Clinton, the dignitaries, and the throngs, as well as the "millions" of dancers dressed as butterflies, doves, puppets, and fish making ready for the great O.C. entrance. Of course, I couldn't carry a bullet in my pocket. Barney would have been "in-censed."

I was dropped off, along with my mate, who was a young college coed who looked like a hockey player, at a door marked AOB, which stood for Atlanta Olympic Broadcasting (in some cases the "O" stood for obnoxious). My supervisor, Robert, said, "Only those with a 5, an O, or a green sticker, or a red sticker, or a computerized strip on their badge can enter. I'll check with you later." I'll bet you will, I thought, smirking.

Nonetheless, I searched the badges valiantly, of those who entered, trying to see the numbers, stickers, and strips, wondering on occasion if I was letting someone in who might attack the president, or an indiscriminate butterfly. By an hour or so later, it became such a blur of humanity, I was just grinning at the hordes who went in and out my door. Godzilla could have lumbered in and I would have just given him a wink.

Dinnertime relief came none too soon – a sandwich, salad, and Coke, while sitting in a tent across the street in the back of the stadium with scores of frazzled volunteers. When I returned to my post, I had been moved a few yards down in the lower bowels of the stadium to the "police and press entrance," where some five million city, county, armed services, and secret service police personnel, as well as press and photographers entered and exited.

For the next four or five hours, great hordes of dancing butterflies, fish, and children/puppets passed up and down the corridor. Police of various size and shape passed in and out for smoke breaks, potty breaks and motorcycle breaks. The French press persons asked where "commentary" was, whatever that meant. Peruvian camera men asked where Peru was. A butterfly asked where the puppets went.

At one point, I wasn't sure where anyone was supposed to go, while standing there in a daze with my badge, in my green pants and Jungle Jim pith helmet. My security mate moved her arms with authority, saying, "Follow this corridor on around, you will find it," pointing her arm like a hockey stick. Yeah, I thought, if you don't end up on Marietta Street.

On one of my few breaks, I did get to go up and see some of the Opening Ceremonies and took a few pictures with my pocket camera. I caught the red costumes intersecting with the green costumes, as the butterflies circled the puppets. I saw a big white dude hand off the torch to Evander Holyfield, who disappeared among the fish.

Back at my post, the big torch bearer, white dude passed by looking for the restroom. I pointed, wanting to ask him who he was, but didn't have the nerve. By then, I didn't have the nerve to do much of anything. He was probably some game show host.

So, by around 1:00a.m. I began trudging up the street with the other five billion dazed and drowsy spectators toward MARTA for my ride out to darkened suburbia. While working at my "security assignment," I was unable to see the final ceremonies and asked the couple walking next to me, "Who finally lit the big Olympic flame?"

"Ich mon troug bztfe gogfn," the man answered. Okay, so a few steps later, I asked another man who lit the torch.

"Esta usted como seimpre mucho knowo nothingo," he stammered.

Not giving up my quest, I approached a third man. "Sir, do you speak English?" – a question I never thought I would have to ask in Atlanta.

He did, though he was from Colombia, South American, and told me it was Mohammad Ali, as he disappeared in the maddening crowd. Appropriate, I thought. The "Greatest," is still the "Greatest."

So, my first night on post at the bottom of the stadium had ended, and the much anticipated Games began, along with my lumbago.

BEWARE THE SECURITY MEASURE OF SEARCHING THROUGH THE ABYSS WITHIN A WOMAN'S PURSE

(You could get bitten)

To begin with, I lost my stadium job. It wasn't that disappointing to have another "security" assignment, but I had not planned on searching patrons with a wan or a Geiger counter, for that matter. What was an inside job, pointing toward the restroom, now became a "search and seize" job, if you dared seize whatever it was you searched.

So, now I was outside at the gate entrance on the west side of the interstate, some distance from the stadium. Technically, I was still "assigned to the stadium area," but the term, "area" had a new meaning. I found myself standing under a tarp covering at a table, my arm plunged deep into a woman's "duffel" bag-purse, all the way up to my elbow.

If you know me at all, you know I am long of arm and "up to my elbow" is some distance, as I rummaged around in the abyss of purse depth. As Barney might instruct Otis and Gomer, "Now men, no bag can go unsearched."

The dear woman tourist/person said, wryly, "Be careful."

"Huh?" I grunted, fumbling through wrapped sandwiches and unmentionables.

"You might get bit," she clucked with a smile. I quickly retrieved my arm and said with my best security smile, "You're clean." I wanted to add, "but your purse/duffel bag is a dump." But I was cool, kept my southern manners in tact and waved on the New Zealander with the bag full of Izzie dolls.

Early on, they instructed us to "inspect" bags of all types coming through the magnetometer entrance. By Monday of the 2nd week, after the bomb scare downtown, it was "scrutinize, magnetize, and legitimize" each bag. Searching through bags at the airport check-in gate was mere child's play compared to what we were doing.

"Please have your bags open and ready for inspection," I would blurt out as they prepared to enter through the metal gate. As they got to me, up on the table plops shopping bags, paper bags, plastic bags, camera bags, duffel bags, sports bags, shoulder bags, picnic bags, waist packs, tummy packs, fanny packs, back packs, and Army packs.

In each bag and pack was more paraphernalia than space permits me to mention. Suffice to say, searching for "unsuspecting contraband" became the least of my worries. Getting my hand out safely from the mess within was paramount.

Clearly, nothing of any size, shape, nor zipper proportion can equal the plethoric number of items jammed, crammed, or otherwise clanging amongst each other within the recesses of a woman's purse. When the woman told me – even with a grin – that something might bite me, I most assuredly believed her.

Each purse seemed to have its own sea of murky, five-and-dime/flee market contents. It was as if they stormed the door of the store/market and worked their way up and down every aisle, picking and purchasing every item in sight and shoving it among the pile, thinking they might need it sometime during their visit to the Games.

Hairpins, bobby pins, safety pins, ball point pens, play pens. Note pads, corn pads, nail pads, foot pads, and other pads I shouldn't mention. Charge cards, playing cards, identification cards, bus cards, pledge cards. (Some were Baptists, what can I say?) Hardback novels, paperback novels, magazines, brochures, schedules, National Inquirers, coupon savers. Kleenex, handkerchiefs, paper towels, cloth towels, wet ones open, wet ones closed, and dry ones, two-days-old.

And all this was on top, in view. There was the infamous second layer...which covered make-up, compacts, lipstick, lip gloss, lips chapped, toothpaste, tooth brush, and perfume and cologne of every scent imaginable, even Hungarian. Hair brushes, hair pieces, hair combs, hair picks, hair nets, hair spray, and hair balls. The search went on through the night, through the abyss.

On very few occasions, I would notice a woman come through with no purse. This was a strange, yet sad phenomenon. Usually, she was trailing her family. There was a blank stare on her face, knowing she was out in public, for some time, I might add, without her "life" hanging over her shoulder.

Perhaps thinking of the safety factor, she probably left it in the trunk of the car, a normal secure place. I could tell, though, that she was totally out of sync and would have to depend on her family to "carry" her through the day's experiences. A trip to the restroom for her could be devastating. I could imagine her standing blandly in front of the mirror, with nothing to do…no lipstick, no hair pick, no blush, no toothpaste. Just a mere shell of a woman without her purse.

I was glad when my security rummaging into women's purses came to a conclusion, knowing I didn't lose an elbow or even a finger in the process. It did give me cause to be more conscious of the issue. Now I can offer help to my wife when she is searching around through the abyss of her own purse. "Careful, dear, don't get bit."

OLYMPIC EPILOGUE...UGLY HAT BECOMES NEW CREATION

For some reason, Atlanta didn't get the best review for an Olympic site. We had enough glitches, I suppose, for the head Games commentator, Bryan Gumble to "grumble" about. There were enough interviews with Carl Lewis, the aging fastest man who knew this was his last, to save for track and field archives. There was enough yelling at the crowd by winning runners, crying for more and more adulation from the throngs of spectators, to ruin 100,000 pairs of ears.

By the end of the first week, I had watched enough on TV to never want to see another pretty synchronized leg pointing skyward from the water, never see another big, tall NBA basketball team beat up on another poor short team from Equador, and never see another silly looking "Izzie" doll. And, my "volunteer" days are over...no more searching bags, pointing at rest rooms, nor wear a Jungle Jim helmet again. In a word, it will become a creative lampshade.

Quite understandably, the event that became more newsworthy than Michael Johnson's gold lame` running shoes, was the bomb blast in Centennial Park. Poor Richard Jewel's ordeal ended after finally getting the FBI to believe his story of non-involvement, to the point where he sued and won for his treatment. Good for him.

What else can be said about the Atlanta's Olympics of 1996? Two lines: one by former news show hostess, Linda Ellerbe, "And so it goes," and two, from the great Walter Cronkite, "And that's the way is was." So it was and so it's gone.

PART IV

**FAMILY TREES ARE GETTING OUT ON A LIMB,
PARENTAL CHANGES, OTHER INSTRUCTIONS,
AND MAMA'S BRAND OF HUMOR**

FAMILY TREES OF
THE "STEP" VARIETY

Back when President "Billy Jeff" Clinton was in the White House, there was some investigative reporting which indicated that the "good ship lollipop's" captain had a rather interesting family tree. We knew mostly of his mother, married more than once and about his half brother, Rodger, a not-so-famous musical entertainer.

We also know, that as time went on, another issue in and around the Pennsylvania Avenue address became a bit more interesting and his family tree took a back seat. It is not my intention in this essay to bring up that many sided and sordid episode.

Nonetheless, if someone decides to make a run for the high and lifted up seat of the presidency, you can bet that the "no family stone unturned" investigative press will find out about the third cousin twice removed whose step-mother had triplets by her second husband who happens to deliver mail in the mountains of Montana and is married to a descendent of the Blackfoot tribe out of south Helena.

Truth be known, most of us are of the "un-scrutinized family variety," with our own skeletons in the closet, and simply try not to bring up the possibility of a Christmas visit from the Montana cousin Harley, his Indian wife, Mary Little-Toe and the triplets.

Personally, my family may have been pretty normal. Some people who know me might ask me to define "normal," but defining "boring" might be a bit more appropriate as it relates to the description of my family tree. Outside of a few modern era divorces, it's nothing to go overboard scrutinizing.

But it has caused me to think that there is a cultural development in our society which is going to stretch our future family trees way beyond the basic spreading chestnut tree patterns. Connecting with past kin, ex-kin, future-kin, and step-kin is going to become a family scrapbook menagerie.

Let me give you an example. Suppose John and Mary divorce. They have a boy child who grows up, marries, and he and his wife have a child. After a few years, the mother and father of that child decide to divorce. The child lives with his mother, who sometime later, marries a second time. And, as you might imagine, his father marries again, also.

Are you with me? Okay, let's go visit the grandparents. His paternal grandparents were John and Mary, remember? But they divorced long ago and have since remarried and this makes four...a real grandmother and a step-grandfather, and a real grandfather and step-grandmother.

Meantime, the child's mom has two parents who are his maternal grandparents. But they also have divorced and remarried, which means he now has eight, adding two more step-grandparents. But remember that his mom remarried and his step-dad's parents became another set of step-grandparents.

And his father remarried and his step-mom, (father's wife) also brings to the marriage two parents, who become his step-grandparents, too. What this kid has now is about 150 grandparents and step-grandparents, thrice removed to the third power. The only good thing about it might be Christmas presents.

On top of this, add the number of the other cousins, nephews, uncles and aunts of the "step" and "ex" variety, and you have the makings of a family tree large enough to find a significant place in the sequoia forests of California. This kid is probably his own second cousin, giving the old song, "I'm My Own Grandpa" a new meaning altogether.

Keep the home fires burning and the pot on the stove. Never know who might "step" up to your front door.

A SYMPHONIC ZEPPELIN TOOK THIS FATHER BACK TO THE "ROCK" FUTURE

To be honest, I am not much of a classical symphony connoisseur, but will on occasion try to get a bit of "couth."

One summer night in the 90s, my wife and I found ourselves at Chastain Park amphitheater in north Atlanta where the summer breezes blew gently at the onset of dusk. The air was filled with a cacophony of murmuring from the laid-back crowd, hovering in small groups around tables, munching, drinking, and enjoying each other's company. It was a perfect night for the symphony to tune up once more under the cloudless sky.

But on this night, only if you were a rock music fan! No Beethoven's 5th or Star Spangled Banner crescendo on this night. No white ties and tails, either. The symphony members were in T-shirts, splashed with psychedelic colors on front and back. On this night, they plied a different tune, tapped their feet to a "different drummer," producing weirder tunes, louder tunes, Baby Boomer tunes, tunes that this crowd cut their "rock and roll" teeth on.

On this night we got the "Zeppelin...*Led Zeppelin,*" a vintage rock (perhaps a contradiction of terms) band of the 70s youth. Most parents of their generation – me included, now senior adults and of a different era - might think a Led Zeppelin would be a misnamed, misguided, incorrigible dirigible, not long to be skyward.

But if you had a Baby Boomer and suffered through their "rock years," you probably know the name and realize it was their version of Guy Lumbardo gone bust.

So, how do I, aging music lover that I am, know this? Well, from my own young Baby Boomer whom I once "begat," of course. But let me go further back, which reminds me of what my band director told me in my 8th grade trombone class...as in, "go further back, Mason!"

60

In the 50s, during my college days, I became a rock fan when rock wasn't cool. When I heard Bill Haley and the Comets do "Rock Around The Clock" for the first time, I knew I was hooked. That was followed by Fats Domino singing "I'm Walkin'," Little Richard warbling "Good Golly, Miss Molly," and Elvis strutting out "Don't You Step On My Blue Suede Shoes." I even had my own blue suede shoes. I was cool, man!

In high school, I had been musically sheltered, dancing to the likes of Perry Como, Patti Page, Rosemary Clooney, and Johnny Ray. I needed a change. Naturally, rock music was not well thought of, to put it mildly, and so, I kept my rock music interests "in the closet," where it remained until much later in life. Even during my seminary days while training for the ministry, I never so much as hummed "You Ain't Nothin' But A Hound Dog" on campus, lest I was caught and brought before the dean of anti-rock.

The years passed on and I sojourned throughout the land. One day, my young son became a teenager – a trick which God plays on know-it-all, hiding-in-the-closet, naïve parents. One day he was a cherubic 12-year-old Boy Scout. And then, almost overnight, we heard it…"BRAAAANNGGGG BOOM, BOOOOM, BOOOOM, YEEEE-AAAARRRGG…YEAH, YEAH, YEAH"…this sound, emanating from the closet, then the bedroom, and blasting out into the hallway toward the heavens.

This was, as many other innocent parents would testify, my introduction to Led Zeppelin and his other minions around 1973. My life, to say nothing of the teen-person's life who once lived in the bedroom, has not been the same since. There were other odd-sounding names like ZZ Top, Jethro Tull, and Rolling Stones, who all sounded like the convulsions of the seven-headed horse coming out at Armageddon in the book of Revelation.

What ever happened to Fats and Bill and Little, and my life of rock in the 50s, I wondered to myself. It's a blur, history, it came out of the closet and left me. Which is what my teenage resident did. Now he's a father and is dealing with his own "teen-person" and her style of music. Life goes on. He doesn't even own a set of drums any more. He has a real job.

But for that one night in the park, the symphony in psyche-delic attire did old Zeppelin proud and I reminisced of my own "rock" years, and my son's rock years and actually remembered a couple of tunes, wandering back to the "BRAAANG – BOOM" from the upstairs bedroom of the 70s.

And I yelled, and whistled, and shouted "bravo" to the long-haired singer on stage and the versatile Atlanta Symphony backing him up, and perhaps, just a time or two that evening, I wished for that time years ago, listening, even with deafening ears, to the beat of the kid's drums upstairs.

IF MOTHERS ARE FROM VENUS, THEN FATHERS MUST BE FROM WAYCROSS, GEORGIA

Toward the end of the 20th century, there was a lot of gibber-jabber surrounding the book that asserted "women were from Venus and men were from Mars," meaning men are "from another planet." It postulated, pontificated and opinionated about the differences between men and women and the way they approach life and make decisions about, say, purchasing stock or just who should kill the roach in the bathtub.

Admittedly, I decided not to read about something which is and has always been as plain as the nose on one's face – that the female has always made the decisions about who is trading stock, who deals with roaches, and who takes a bite out of an apple. This has been going on since the beginning of time. Just think about the apple, thank you.

I would like, however, to take this issue to another level…the difference in the way mothers do mothering, as opposed to the way fathers do fathering, or seemingly, stumble around trying to make sense out of their responsibilities. Mostly, moms have seen to it that kids have a big plate of hot nourishing food for supper, help them practice their cursive writing, fix boo-boos, and put clean sheets on the bed.

Dads on the other hand, give the kid a mitt the size of a garbage can lid, tell him or her to squeeze the ball into the glove, using the other little biddy hand to hold it in place. We don't want you to cause your team to lose the World Series in a few years, do we, son! This was part of the "old days" of mothering and fathering. Today, mothers are still from Venus but fathers are from somewhere close to Waycross, Georgia, figuratively speaking.

Years back, lifestyles began to change and moms started going to work, but still cooked supper and helped with cursive and boo-boos. Dad still did baseball when he came home from work. It went further. Now, Dad fixes lunches, makes the bed, and takes one kid across town to a magnet school, while Mom gets the diaper bag and the wee-est one and drops her off at the day care center. Both are at work by 9:00.

Or, Mom leaves at 7:00a.m. for the law firm downtown and Dad fixes breakfast, gets the kids off to school, stays home and vacuums, answering to the newest handle, "Mr. Mom" and the new "Venus" mom may come home and after the supper that he cooks, help the kids with their soccer exercises.

It occurred to me one Father's Day back in the 90s that after fathering for almost forty years, it's still somewhat of a mystery as to what it is that I should have done or should now be doing. Through the years, I provided food, clothing, and shelter. But basically, I was just following the rules. The father who doesn't follow the basics is a lout, jerk, runaway, or maybe in jail. But most fathers do more than the basics.

A good father protects, instructs how to watch out for cars, puts the worm on the hook, teaches the use of seat belts, sees to it that they mow the yard, preaches against drugs, goes to church on Sundays, and explains the importance of buying good insurance.

So, what happens? They dart across four lanes without looking, chose to bungie-jump rather than the more sedentary sport of fishing, drive with one hand while talking into the other, test the limits of bad habits, think church is for sissies, and don't buy enough insurance to cover any of the above.

Yet another thing fathers do that seems to be part of their "way out," as in Waycross make-up, is give advice.

I suppose I have given mounds of advice through the years to my two offspring and I suppose I will continue till they close the casket and put me under, or open the urn and let me fly, whichever. We fathers have a quiver full of advice-isms which can pierce the air at a moments notice.

Problem is, no one wants it. Here is a man with years of experience driving a car, mowing the lawn, selecting ties, discussing multiple topics with the opposite sex, setting digital clocks, and changing flat tires. Does anyone above or below the age of 20 want any of this valuable advice? Absolutely not! Why did I learn how to parallel park between two other cars, and mow in a square rather than by rows, and share my inner most secrets on cooking chili with their mother, if I wasn't going to share said advice with *them* as they grow up?

And then, of course, there's another item fathers must provide if we're worth our salt. And that is money! Unlike advice, children will take money on the spot, without questioning or frowning or hesitating. Fathers must be good "providers" of mucho dinero! The idea came over on the Mayflower. Maybe it was already here among the native Americans. "Um, big brave want-um happy tee-pee...better get much wampum!"

So, I guess the good father from "Waycross" provides the basics of food, clothing and shelter, gives sound advice whether they want it or not, knows where the insurance agent is at all times, and has plenty of money.

And by the way, honk when you drive through Venus and don't sit under the apple tree with anybody...period!

COULD WE EVER
OVERDOSE ON INSTRUCTIONS?

Ever since I was old enough to understand "No, No," I have been receiving instructions about everything from flossing to slouching. Those who imparted these instructions are varied in background...mother ("Be careful driving back and forth, there are a lot of idiots out there"), wife ("Never throw away the box you want to take something back to the store in"), and various aunts, teachers, police persons, preachers, and even children just to mention a few.

Outside the range of such sagely advisors, there is yet another group. These are former politicians who went to jail and lived to write about it, former IRS accountants who wrote a book about how to arrange your form 1040 to stay out of jail, or the former preacher who messed up his 1040, did go to jail, but afterward became a talk-show host.

Even I, writer of the Mason Jar, once told my readers not to talk to yourself while driving down the street because the man in the pick up in the next lane may think you're cussing him and shoot at you.

You would think that after years of being blessed with so many instructions that we would be up to our ear lobes in bits of wisdom. Not so, or to use the idiotic expression of our youthful culture..."Not!"

During the mid-90s, while doing some Christmas shopping at a book store, I noticed yet another book of instructions which came forth and the little sucker (small and hardly more than 50 pages) became a big time seller. It was called, appropriately, *Life's Little Instruction Book.* Clever, huh?

Every writer worth his or her typewriter is muttering, "Why didn't I think of that?" And the reason is because it sold 3 million copies the first year and made the author, a man named Jackson Brown, Jr., rich, at least rich for a writer.

Among the instructions in the book were these two..."*take a nap on Sunday afternoon*" and "*eat prunes!*" Not necessarily in that order, I would gingerly offer. My opinion, as opposed to instruction, is that if you eat too many prunes beforehand, you may not finish your nap, if you understand what I mean. I pay "tribute" to the glorious prune later in this book and you can be the judge. But I appreciate his endorsement of prunes as a source of good health, instructionally speaking.

Then, he took things further a year or so later and published another such instruction book entitled, *Live, Learn, And Pass It On*. What this means in writer language is, if I can paraphrase here, "In my lifetime, I (Mr. Brown) have learned a lot of instructions from people here and there and I want you to buy this book and give it to somebody." I might add, that's not a bad idea for the Mason Jar book, but I won't be presumptuous. I should be thankful you've gotten this far, if you have, reminding myself of a wise instruction of yesteryear, "A book in the hand is worth two on the shelf!"

In his second book, Brown mentions something that might be questionable in the truest "instructional" sense. He wrote, "You can't hide a piece of broccoli in a glass of milk." Now in my considered opinion that this is as plain as the nose on your face. It doesn't mean that you should *not* place a piece of broccoli in the glass to try to hide it. It merely states, if you are trying to get broccoli off your plate, don't put it in your milk.

His point here may be in the category of instruction, but it really is a fact. But in the scheme of things, it doesn't really matter, does it. I'm just wonding if anyone ever suggested this bit of wisdom to President George Bush I, before he sent out a decree in the early 90s on the subject of broccoli.

You remember, he once placed an order – not *for* broccoli, but *against* broccoli -uttering, "henceforth and ever more, there would be no broccoli on my First Plate," or words to that affect. Did he, in fact, try to hide his broccoli in a glass of milk while responding to the first chef, "Read my lips…there is no broccoli on my plate?"

Maybe he'll tell us in his memoirs.

MEMORIES OF MAMA'S
"UNSUBTLE" BRAND OF HUMOR

"Seems like one doctor after another is
the way we live – makes me sick!"

And speaking of those instructions you just read about, we'll agree that mothers, perhaps more than anyone, have a certain style for getting their message across. Most times it's blunt, no nonsense and in your face, like, "If you leave this house looking like that, forget meals and lodging, and look for us somewhere in South Dakota."

They can also be subtle. The still single, 33-year-old son makes the obligatory Mother's Day call and asked the equally obligatory question, "How you doing, Mom?" She answers with stabbing innuendo, "Oh fine. I've been over at your Aunt Lil's, playing with her *four grandchildren!*"

My mother could "say the darnedest things," to use the phrase. She lived in Western Kentucky all of her adult life. After my dad died, she and I began a regular Sunday afternoon long distance phone conversation, sort of a verbal rendition of the old "Letter to Mama" on the old Carson show. And for some reason she became more humorous in her latter years.

After dispensing a plethora of blunt, as well as subtle messages to Dad and me, she probably figured the only thing left to do was laugh. One such Sunday, a visiting preacher had been at her church. "Who?" I asked. "Well," she answered, "I can't remember his name. Must notta been much good, else I'd remembered who he was."

There was always the issue of hearing. She would forget her hearing aid often. I asked once if she could hear me okay, and she answered, "Not well. My hearing aid is in the refrigerator. If I'd had it this morning in Sunday School, I might've learned something."

Driving was always an issue that I worried about. And she had a little fender- bender once, and worried out loud, "I been driving since 16 and never had an accident and now this. I'm 80 years old now and that's what worries me." I guess if I thought of it very long, I could be worried at my age, but I won't dwell on it.

She once admitted that she had "dropped" recently regarding her dress size. "I'm sixteen at one end, eighteen at the other and maybe something else in the middle."

And one Sunday afternoon she told me that her "eyes seemed to be okay, but I'm gonna have to change my glasses."

I'm glad I took time to write down some of her "mamaisms." I found through the years that as we children get older, we discover that our parents become much more blunt in their latter years. Subtlety becomes a thing of the past.

She spent her last three years in a nursing home, or as I would *bluntly* call it, the "holding cell." We had picked this home beforehand, "just in case." We hoped she would never have to go, of course. After strolling through on our initial, look-see trip, she had seen enough to remark, "Let's get outta the hands of the vultures." Not much subtlety there.

Nevertheless, she finally ended up languishing away with them and after physical and mental deterioration, her body gave up and the phone calls from Mama came to an end. Now, I pray, she's playing the piano in heaven for Dad. I don't know how God works that out, but I'm confident a piano she loved so is up there somewhere.

My mother's blunt humor seeps through as I speak of her last, rather unqualitative years of life. Most of us who've experienced a parent's existence in such surroundings finally throw subtlety to the wind, and in '96, I spent my first Mother's Day without her. It didn't seem right without a phone call and a few laughs. But the memories remain.

And as family fate would have it, my Aunt Ree – who rivaled Mama for best cook of the family, and who finds herself in a similar state, entered into the 21st century pushing toward 100 and we still talk on the phone on Sundays. That's another story.

As I suggested at the very beginning of this section, family trees sometimes have long limbs and some branches are like the bunny...they just keep on going. So, enjoy all the family life and breadth and depth you possibly can.

PART V

AGING, ACHING, FORGETTING, AND A BOX OF CHOCOLATES

**If Robert Browning's "best is yet to be,"
why does mine feel like it's already been?**

JUST HOW OLD DOES ONE HAVE TO BE IN ORDER TO QUALIFY TO BE "OLD?"

Somewhere in the middle of the "nines," I began to ask myself the question...When does one become "old." When I was a kid, everyone was old, especially my adult family.

My grandparents, for example, seemed old to me. But they still canned corn and washed in the old black pot in the wash house. Grandpa milked and worked in the tobacco field while he spit his "baccy" and Grandma took me fishing back on Plum Creek and now I'm not sure you're "old" when you do things like bending over and stomping through the fields.

About this time of ponderous thinking, I visited my two aunts who had been living together since the early 40s. Thinking about their aging state of being on the "cusp of their 90s," I asked about any plans they had made for selling the house and moving to an apartment, as others their age had done. The younger one batted her eyes, and responded, "Well, I 'speck we'll have to do something about that when we get old." If I remember, we immediately changed the subject.

A dear senior adult visited me one day at the church house. She had moved from Decatur and was living in another part of Atlanta, closer to her children. She lamented that the new church she joined wasn't too exciting. I suggested that she attend a senior adult group similar to the "Young At Heart" at our church. "Oh, they're old!" Then she chuckled and added, "I'm just 86, you know!" I suppose, to her, 86 wasn't "old."

I know people in their forties who seem old, but I'm sure they don't think so. And if you get to be 50 you can join the AARP, but does that "milestone" make one old?

I must admit that I have an AARP card, which means that I am past 50. Am I old? It's a dangerous thing to admit one's age, especially during the latter years of one's life, and it's mainly because we don't want people to think we're "old."

During the 90s, I happened to "cross the great divide" as some may say. Maybe I was old then, but a lot of people say I'm old now. I keep saying to myself that I don't look "old." Some of my well-wishing friends say, "dream on." Well, I don't feel *that* old. Most of the time. At least every other day. Especially in the middle of the day. Nothing before 9 a.m. and after 10 p.m. counts at this age, does it? I just decided that I don't feel old between 9 a.m. and 10 p.m. After that, it's anybody's guess, huh?

I remember thinking as a teenage that 40 years of age was so far off I wouldn't get there. We had communist China, the Russians, the bomb shelters and Elvis doing a "whole lot of shakin'." Doomsday mentality made me think, naah, I'll never make it. Then when I was 30, I thought "retirement" was so far off that I wouldn't make it either. Maybe I wouldn't make 55 or 60, or, heaven help me, 65!

But lo, 2000 came and I surrendered, retired, and I passed over the "heaven help me" age. Old? I'm not so sure at all. Now, it's a matter of perspective, an attitude, one of those "Ah-ha!" moments in our lives when you realize you're only "as old as you think you are." And for some reason, I don't think I are old!

After retirement, my wife and I decided to join a church closer to our home.

We visited a Sunday School class, "for our age-group." (That phrase has gotten a lot of ministers in trouble). Afterward, walking down the hall to church, I muttered softly, "These people are older than we are." As we rounded the corner toward the sanctuary, I passed a mirror, and glanced at myself, just to see if my tie was straight and my sport coat was still where I had left it earlier – on my shoulders. My glance told me what I really didn't want to know. I muttered softly to my wife once more, "Lord honey, I look just like they do."

But am I old? No. Depressed, yes, but not old. Never!

REMEMBERING WHAT I FORGOT
CAN BE EMBARRASSING

GOLF TALE: A golfer began to have trouble seeing the ball at a distance. He shared this one day with a friend, who said, "I have good eye-sight. I'll go with you and be your eyes, so to speak." Next day, the golfer hit the ball off the tee a goodly distance. The other man drove the cart along the fairway for some time and finally the golfer asked, "Where did the ball go?" He friend responded, "I don't remember."

I forgot about writing the letter. Actually I couldn't remember if I had already written it or not. Like taking pills after breakfast. You saw them on the table earlier but after breakfast, you're walking away and wondering to yourself, "Did I take my pills?"

It was a perplexity. Do I write the letter as if I hadn't written and take a chance that I hadn't? Or do I write the letter and admit I may have forgotten, so here's another one. The recipient would mutter, "Hey Mavis, ole Joe is losing it. He wrote another letter about the trip. Same stuff." If I take the first route and I had written a letter, well, it's a dilemma, to say nothing of embarrassing.

What this means is I can't remember if I already wrote the thank you note for the Christmas tree ornament the boss's wife gave us, or the condolence note to friends for the loss of their family cat, or the congratulations note to the neighbor's kid for winning the Girl Scout cookie sell-out.

My dear aunt suggested that I keep a record of notes that I write. Well that sounds like a good idea, until you forget to write down in your "note log" a note that you wrote the note. If you notice that it's been sometime since your last entry, you begin to wonder if you missed noting a record about the note. You see the predicament.

Forgetting is a common ailment. Like, the car keys, the billfold, the meeting, where we parked the car, the kids, and sometimes a very important name. Two couples were dining together and one man asked the other man if they had seen any movies lately. "Yeah, we went the other night...uh, what was that...uh, er, - he paused and asked, "What flower has thorns and red petals?" The first man answered, "A rose."

The man turned to his wife and asked, "Rose, what was that movie we saw last week?"

Tell you something worse. One Sunday afternoon I was taking a siesta and, while slumbering slightly with my eyes closed, I suddenly remembered something I forgot that I should have remembered days ago. What happened when I remembered was the same response that's happened before, following such thoughts of remembering in panic. There is a sudden rush of endorphins and molecules or whatever those things are that run through your blood stream, rushing to get somewhere.

When they are through rushing, the blood flow slows down and you stare at the wall and say, "Uh, oh," a phrase which the writer, Robert Fulghum, parleyed into a best selling book of the same name and means, generally, that you're about to be submerged in "deep tapioca."

What had pierced my brain waves that had been forgotten by said waves up to that nap-time point was a very important date. I had absentmindedly forgotten it to such an extent that *five days* had passed since the date, which meant, in husband terms, "Man, I may *really* be in deep tapioca!"

I forgot our wedding anniversary! February 25 somehow came and went, blissfully. What a bad husband-person I am. What an old, dilapidated, broken-down brain I have. Gone way beyond "senior moments" to "senior days!"

So, maybe it was the Leap-Year Syndrome, I mused to myself. We were married in 1984, a Leap Year, and I had some idiotic notion that if you married during a Leap Year, you didn't have to observe such an anniversary but once every four years. Sounds logical to me, huh?

And, George Orwell wrote a book of the same number, predicting among other things, that "Big Brother" would be watching and deciding for us at so many turns that surely the "system" would remind us not only to pay our property tax on time, but to remember your anniversary, dummie! But alas, not everything in his book came true, and poor citizen husband that I am, it is up to me and my own wits to remember this important date.

How do I approach this predicament without scrambled egg on my face. More than that, what form of recompense will have to be meted out for such anniversary treason. A new car? A diamond necklace? Re-paper the bathroom? Perhaps we could sit down and discuss the situation as two mature adults. This has been a busy month, time-consuming projects, unbearable stress. I mean, I was at the point of even admitting that I am getting old and forgetful, a dastardly nasty admission for any "older" husband.

Or maybe I could approach it as a loving husband, gently suggesting the many ways "I love thee," counting out the smile that is one-in-a-million, her beautiful appearance when we go out, her endless trips to the grocery for my provisions and nourishment. The disturbing thing was, she had not said one word about it.

So, that night at the table while filling myself with her succulent mashed potatoes, I broached the subject. "Honey, do you know what I forgot last week, my sweet poopsie?"

"No, what?" she replied.

"I forgot Tuesday," I said, with as wimpy a look as I could muster with potatoes on my lip. She paused a moment, then gave me a shocking expression, mouth a-gape.

Sometimes, the good Lord, in His infinite watch care over the feeble-minded and brain-impaired, smiles His blessing upon us when we least deserve it.

She had forgotten, too.

THE OLDER WE GET, THE HARDER IT IS TO CHANGE HABITS

Exa: If you make a conscious decision to get more exercise and take up cross-country skiing, make sure it's a small country.

Lewis Grizzard, the syndicated southern columnist, finally succumbed to his bad heart in the mid-90s. He gave it the good-old-boy try, having been incarcerated in the hospital for several operations with the very best of medical assistance.

I think he knew, like most of us, that he had developed some habits along life's road that possibly had some effect on his "ticker." The Atlanta paper noted at one point early on that ole Lewis needed to "change his habits," particularly his love for barbecue, cheese grits, and eggs over easy so "the yellow crawls," as he so eloquently put it.

Admittedly, I have had some experience with heart struggles. A little bit in my genes, but probably most of it coming from bad eating habits. The doctors give us their "best shot" at our problem whether it's surgery or advice, but most times it's followed with a line like, "And you're going to have to change your way of life." Which means, you better *change your habits* if you want to keep breathing.

We are all guilty of having one or more habits we should change, the results of which would make us "a better person for it," as crazy Richard Simmons might intone, while urging a hefty person to kick higher in order to be a less hefty person. But if you've tried to play the habit game, it's harder than writing a term paper on the life and times of Chaucer for English Lit 101.

For example, during the time I would be writing this piece, usually on a Sunday afternoon, I give way to the habit of going to the kitchen for a little snack. I say little, because I feel somewhat guilty if I go get a big snack. In other words, I struggle more with my habit if I have a whole plate with a big snack on it, than a little plate with a small snack on it.

77

What happens - because of my habit - is that during the time of writing one of my columns, I go get a snack...several times. I make trips to the kitchen once for graham crackers, then one later for a banana, one for a few peanuts, one for a coke and so on. I feel better doing this rather than loading up, er, uh, I mean, procuring tidbits all at once.

This is a habit I developed over the years while writing for the Decatur News Era, gazing out the window, trying to form sentence structure, while wondering what I should eat, er, uh, I mean, write next. It's not that any of these snacks are individually bad for you per se. It's merely the volume of said snacks that brings the habit to fruition, shall we say. So, I need to change this habit of volume snacking if I don't want to look as big as Senator Ted Kennedy one day. I'll mull on it, as I'm sure he does.

I have other habits that I ought to change, such as starting a sentence and pausing until next Thursday to finish it. Don't know how this got started. Talking to too many doctors, I suppose. You start to tell them what the problem is, and all of a sudden they leave the little cubicle and come back two days later.

I'll have to change this habit, for I fear that one day my dear wife may stand at the door with her bags in hand and say, reproachfully, "Unless you finish that sentence, I'm leaving on Tuesday before you finish it Thursday." I need a speech therapist.

Part of my responsibility of past years with Senior Adult ministries has included bus tours to various and sundry places. It has been my practice to "preach" punctuality regarding bus leaving times. And generally folks have pretty well returned on time, at least, "close enough for country," as the musicians say.

Once, however, a lady on her first trip returned 30 minutes late and we "had prayer for her" and gave her the "last-person-on-the-bus" round of applause. From then on, she was always near the head of the line. Her husband said I did in one trip what he's tried to change for 40 years. But then, he wasn't driving the bus.

Of course, one can change habits if one has the right incentives. Too many speeding tickets will finally get your attention to slow down. Teachers with large size rulers will change your habits of talking in class. And wives standing at the door with their bags packed can cause one to start finishing sentences more quickly.

Guess it's time for my mid-hourly snack. Some habits are more difficult to adjust than others. My doctor says I ought to mull on it, especially at my age, if Browning's "yet to be" gets to be any better.

YOU NEVER KNOW
WHAT YOU'LL GET FROM THAT
VALENTINE'S BOX OF CHOCOLATES

Valentine's Day comes around annually and whomps us right smack in the mouth...literally! It has simply gotten out of hand and into mouth.

Now, before you think me a "scrooge," I am all for this day for lovin' and huggin' and kissin' and poopsie talk to your best sweetie pie and your cutesie wutsie, who are, hopefully, one and the same.

One may go search out just the right card - among the millions of bland to stupid examples - that begins with..."When I look into your eyes, my world spins out of control. Your lips are moist with love, like the lettuce in my salad bowl." Well, I've seen worse!

Or you may send the most expensive roses or daisies or snapdragons, give perfume with the fragrance of kumquats, or dine out elegantly at a posh, quiet, night spot, such as Evans Fine Dining in beautiful Decatur.

But don't – please don't – for the sake of all personkind, don't give a box of chocolates to the one you love, aspire to love, think you might love one day, or just want to love about once a month when the moon is in the seventh phase. Mainly because of what you might *get!*

As you may remember from that 90s' era sage of wisdom, yea verily, Forrest Gump from Greenbow, Alabama, his propitious prognostication about a box of chocolates put this whole Valentine's gift issue into irrefutable perspective. The direct quote came from his dear "Momma," to wit, "Life is like a box of chocolates...you never know what you're gonna ge-yet."

This is precisely my point about this annual heartsie pleasure. Take me, for example. For years, it was my good fortune to wander aimlessly through many a box of chocolates. And believe me, I certainly had no idea what I was getting in the process, other than the ecstatic pleasure of finding the chocolate-covered cherry.

First, I heard that too many boxes of chocolates would rot out my teeth. Wasn't a concern to a ten-year-old, as I raked my hand through the box, scarcely visualizing a toothless grin worse than the Wicked Witch of the West. Even the prospect of my hometown dentist, Dr Kirkpatrick and his faithful assistant, Miss Quarles, drilling in my mouth with a four-inch bore, did not keep me away from numerous coconut and caramel goodies, covered in dark chocolate.

Then, I heard that too much sweet chocolate candy would give you "sugar dibeetus" and you'd dry up and wither away in some indiscriminate rocking chair. No one wanted "sugar dibeetus" but, as I reached for the third chocolate-covered pecan piece, I pictured such a disease among the "old people," figuring I was light-years away from the plight of the prune-juice plagued.

When I became a teenager and Snicker bars were lunch dessert staples, I was told that too many chocolates would give me big "zits" on my nose and other face parts. No teenager in his right mind wants a big, red, painful zit-bump on his or her nose. But Bertie Sue had one on her nose, too, so it didn't matter if we went out together. Pass the box, please.

And, of course, people have said for years, that too many chocolates would make you fat. But being thin of bone through the luck of the genes, I laughed at the fat theory, scarfing down handfuls of chocolate-covered nougats. Perhaps fat was a plague to many a woman who loves Whitman's Special Valentine Pack, but not me.

Then, my "luck-olate" changed. I found out early in the 90s what Forrest Gump meant about never knowing what you'll get. You can get your *cholesterol* clogged up. Whatever "you ge-yet" in this case, makes your arteries clog up and when I finally had my numbers checked, my cholesterol was so high it had a comma in it. The doctor asked me if I lived at the "Willie Wonka Chocolate Factory."

So, now, it seems a bit unfair and even sweetly incongruous – meaning it don't make good sense – for one to give a box of chocolates to one's lovey-poopsie person, realizing that they never know what they'll get...rotten teeth, sugar "dibeetus," big red zits, fatter than a pig at hog-killing time, or the "clogged cholesterol jitters."

Makes Valentine's Day kinda hard to swallow. Pass me a kumquat, please.

GRANDMA MAKES FARM WORK SOUND EASY

Sun comes up every day, hands on the clock tick away,
Looks like our weather's here to stay,
Life's "teegus," ain't it!

Old song

And just when I thought I was aging gracefully, I met this about to be 80-year-old grandmother named Rosemond. She lived on a farm in Western Kentucky "t'other side of Sinking Fork." That's a real place and they had a basketball team we played back in high school days. Just had tobacco farms. Some they cut every August, some they spit on the visiting team in the winter. I supposed it hasn't changed much since.

I was visiting my mama's place called Friendship House for Seniors which she referred to as the "dormitory," in my hometown of Hopkinsville. This was before she went to the "holding cell" I referred to some time back. We were sitting at the dinner table with several others when I began to eavesdrop on the conversation next to me. It was something about canning food on the farm.

"I musta canned 50 quarts of turnip greens, corn, and kraut," said Rosemond, who had come to visit her sister. I soon learned there was more where that came from.

"I fix a big meal every Sunday for my family," she continued. That included, if I remember right, three boys and wives, seven grandchildren, and four great-grandchildren. A daughter also lives down in Georgia and - much to her dismay, I would imagine – cannot make the trip to Grandma's table each Sunday, poor girl.

"You do this every Sunday?" I asked, knowing that I lived in the 90s and that "Sunday dinner" went out with croquet games back about 1955. She nodded.

Ever the observant minister, I asked her about going to church, knowing she had a "heap" of folks coming to her dinner table.

"Oh," she answered matter-of-factly, "I get it ready before Sunday."

Now if you're wondering if this was a soup 'n sandwich affair, think again cafeteria cowboys and cowbettes. This was big time eating. Several vegetables, a couple of meats, biscuits of the non-can variety, and homemade – repeat – homemade pie. "I make several at a time and freeze 'em. Make my own crust, too," she added with some authenticity.

I'm not making this up folks, and there's more. Her husband died some years back, and she maintains the farm. I should have known better than to ask about vegetables. "I grow 'em myself. Till it myself, too. Drive a tractor with my grandson riding with me."

"Your grandson visits?"

"I take care of him. He came a little late after his brother and sister. His mom and dad both work. Rode with his granddad til he was two, and now rides with me."

"Other day," she continued, "I was mowing the yard, (you know of course, that there are no 'cluster home' yards on a farm. Try half an acre), and a storm come up and I just did get finished by supper time. I was about to fix me some eggs, sausage, and biscuits when the power went out. Already had my sausage sliced. So I just ate a bowl of cereal and went to bed."

At some point I muttered something about the cholesterol factor. "Don't know nothing about that." I made some reference to what doctors tell us.

"Well," she said, "I ain't been to a doctor in a long time. Don't know what I got or ain't got."

I thought to myself that they "don't make 'em like" Rosemond any more, even though there are many other men and women in their 80s who are staying active. But there was an everyday spirit about life that this woman shared that was contagious, something that I hope and pray that I can catch in my latter years.

She said one other thing that I remember well, relating to her culinary talents..."I always have a little something sweet." I agree. Everyone needs a "turnip green chaser."

SO WHAT ABOUT A FACE-LIFT TO KEEP FROM LOOKING OLD?

One day about halfway through the "nines," my wife ran in the house after a trip to the mall and quickly turned on the radio, exclaiming, "I want to hear the rest of what this woman says about getting a face-lift."

As most people know, this is a "woman thing" and it is not the first time the subject has popped up in my house. Generally, I grimace and make a husbandly comment, and continue reading the National Geographic article on the effect of lichens on the ocean's bottom. Or is it the effect of the ocean on lichen's bottoms? Whatever.

This time, I paused and in balking fashion, said, "You don't need a face-lift. You don't even have any wrinkles." I wanted her to get the perspective as well as dispel, mainly, any notions of big time financial expenditures. "Well, I might have some day and it's worth thinking about," she retorted.

Later, having looked in the mirror while clipping nose hairs, I muttered, despairingly, "*I*, on the other hand, need a face-lift. I need a hair lift, a wrinkle lift, an eye-sag lift, an Adam's apple lift, and I'm not even down to this root-beer belly." But, of course, most "real" men wouldn't get a face-lift, and if they did, they would never admit it. We just sag. People try to tell us it's okay, 'cause it gives our face "character."

I know only one man, personally, who had a face-lift and he shall remain nameless. I wouldn't want to be the one who gave away his "face secret" and have people say, "So that's what happened to his face! I thought something was wrong." You don't want people to think your face-lift was "wrong," especially afterward.

Naturally, it's become a big business for the people who have money, especially the "stars." Phyllis Diller must get one about every year, with a tack up, er, I mean, touch up each month. I noticed Julie Andrews on television one night and hardly recognized her. She was doing a commercial and was definitely not the same woman who loped through the fields of Austria warbling how alive the hills were with the sound of music.

Sometime later, I noticed Carol Burnett hosting some variety show and she looked like Shirley Temple. Pulled on her earlobe and I think it came off.

And then there's Roseanne. I hesitate to even mention her, but while "surfing" the TV one night, there she was on a talk show with another face. Didn't look like herself and, I might add, anything was an improvement. Would that she could have had a "mouth lift" up over her nose. But I shouldn't be tacky about face-tacking.

I suppose when it's all said and done, a face-lift to make one look better isn't a bad thing, except, of course, if the "liftor" makes a mess of the "liftee." Going under the knife with any surgeon face re-arranger can be a risky business, unless you are absolutely sure he or she knows noses and chinny-chin-chins.

I guess if I wanted to look younger and merely rearranged my face or erased part of it, people who've known me before might come up to me and say, "Joe who?" They may not like my new face. *I* may not like my new face. Looking different after the "lift" is one thing. Looking different and not liking what I'm looking at is another matter altogether. "Could I have some wrinkles back?" is not an optional question.

Reminds me of a night in Lexington, Kentucky back when I was a college sophomore. Sophomores can do some stupid things. As in…I went to a movie with a couple of buddies and decided to dress cool…long argyle socks, Bermuda shorts, and a matching sport coat. Cool, man! I was in style. But then I was also a sophomore.

While waiting in the lobby for the movie to begin, a little boy walked by, paused, and, looking up at me, asked, "Hey, are you a clown?"

Well, I did look different. I was just glad that I could change into something a bit more "cool" when I got back to the dorm. That, of course, is what my college mates strongly suggested.

So, I decided not to dress so "stylish" after that episode, and I guess I'll also keep my wrinkles, thank you. They give me "character."

ABOUT THE WRINKLED PRUNE, THE SCOURGE OF THE FRUIT WORLD

And speaking of wrinkles, it is my studied opinion that prunes have been taking a bad rap for years. True, they aren't the prettiest fruit in the world. They have to compete with the more uppity variety of the fruit world. Who, for example, can resist the succulent orange, the stately apple, the soft, creamy banana, or the popular ruby-red, pile'em-on-your-short-cake strawberry.

But the prune? Well, to be blunt, the suckers are down right ugly. They're sticky, wrinkly, crammed down in a bag, aisles away from all other nice looking fruit of God's creation, save only the raisins and other poor dried fruit variety packs. Even raisins, those little miniature prune-like refugees, are sweeter, come in easy-to-open boxes, and many times are covered in chocolate. There is hardly a better movie snack than a box of chocolate covered raisins. But have you ever seen a chocolate covered prune? No, and I could rest my case here, regarding their plight. But there's more bad prune-news.

They have had a long-standing connection with a very delicate, yet precise issue here and that is, the rather unfortunate association with what I would call one's "body system regularity." It has, embarrassingly, become, er, should I say, the butt of many a joke. The prune and its by-products, in certain quantities, have been known to, let's say, re-regulate your system for you.

I began to understand this fruitful, and perhaps, fateful phenomenon at around the age of ten, one night during supper. Among other things, my mother cooked prunes for the evening meal and for some unknown reason, I "scarfed" down some 22 prunes. My mother remembered the number and never let me forget it. Dad just smiled, knowingly.

Well, she put lots of sugar on them and I liked anything with sugar. She was pretty adept at getting me to eat at least some vegetables by putting sugar on them. Asparagus, turnips, tomatoes, to mention a few. They weren't so hot at age ten, but they were better with sugar on them and so, one night she had prunes and down they went, all twenty-two. And, much to my surprise, I remembered how good they were for about the next three days, if you understand what I mean. The sin of gluttony in the Bible took on a totally new meaning, as I began to understand it in the days following.

And in this connection, prune inventors have, in their "medically proven" wisdom, marketed a derivative of the prune into a product equally known for its "body effect" – prune juice. Though I have never had the nerve to compare, I would suspect it compares in taste to 10-W-30 motor oil. My father, may he rest in peace, swallowed a dangerous amount of coal-oil when he was an overly inquisitive wee child of about two, growing up on the farm, and almost choked to death. Every time he drank prune juice, he said it reminded him of that experience. So, I think I'm close, in comparison.

I mean, you have wonderful, fruity juices to pick from in this world...orange, apple, grape, tropical pineapple, apricot, even tomato juice...so why would anyone decide to pick a fruit juice that tastes like motor oil, for goodness sake? Well, there's only *one* reason, and everyone on God's earth knows what the reason is...*body system regularity.* But that's not all.

I mentioned the wrinkles. This is also a big problem. There is an association here which I will address momentarily, but prunes would be much more appealing if there were no wrinkles, or at least not so many. I remember years ago, in the Dick Tracy comic strip, there was a character who would surface from time to time who was called "Pruneface," poor guy. He would always be dressed up in a suit and tie and his face was full of wrinkles. And they lined his face vertically, not horizontally, which is the way most wrinkles are supposed to appear.

I have wondered a time or two, when I had little else to do but wonder, if eating too many prunes would not only induce an over-abundance of BSR, but also would cause one to develop vertical wrinkles. If so, people might greet you with a, "Hey, you old prune face. How are you?"

How embarrassing to be called by such a name! It's as bad as being called "old chicken neck." And if you're dealing with a bad "chicken neck," you know it would help your image to wear turtleneck sweaters. But when Summer comes, and open collared sport shirts are in season, you are exposed and everyone sees that neck part, flapping back and forth under your chin, blowin' in the wind. Next thing you know, someone sticks you with an embarrassing "neck–of–a–chicken–name."

I've seen a popular preacher on television who has a pretty good amount of chicken neck. It hangs down enough to almost cover the knot on his tie. That's bad enough, but if his wrinkles start going vertical, his preaching days are questionable. There are some features that no make-up job can hide from the camera.

Maybe he could get a "chicken neck lift."

PART VI

FINAL VENTURES OF THE "NINES"
or
It's a bird, mocking loudly...It's a town of silence...It's the pollen blues...and other such pits to dabble in!

A MOCKINGBIRD CONCERT IN THE MIDDLE OF THE NIGHT

This is not about a movie or book of a great lawyer in south Georgia who faced down impossible odds to save a wrongly accused man. Nor is it about the lives of two young kiddos, trying to deal with a guy named "Boo" in the middle of one hot summer.

It is, however, about a mockingbird, high and lifted up in the top of a tree, rendering his (or her) own concert early one morn...very early one morn! And it is about the great consternation which befell me, causing me to bolt straight up in my bed and seriously consider whether I should actually, in the quiet cover of darkness, decide "to kill a mockingbird" or not.

A little background. One night in the spring, when the weather was just right to leave the windows open for fresh breezes, I was startled between slumbers by this mockingbird, doing his (or her) best Rich Little of Birdom routine...a cardinal here, a jay bird there, a brown thrasher yonder. This at around 2:00a.m. in a tree out front just outside our bathroom window. I decided to shut the window and was able to sleep until morning, thankfully.

Next day, I asked my next-door neighbor, "Did you hear the mockingbird last night?" She looked at me as if I was weird, and eased back to her door, saying something about "cleaning the stove."

So, that night, it was hot and we closed the windows all around and had the air conditioning humming, intermittently. Shortly after one in the a.m., we both found ourselves awake and listening to another "concert" by the mockingbird.

Out on the lawn there arose such a clatter, I sprang...you get the picture here. I ran down the hall, through open the front door, stepped out on the stoop and clapped my hands furiously at the tree where "Rich Mockingbird" was in concert. The mocking bird was undeterred - a line I could use in a song, but I won't press it. Anyway, I went back to bed and sat, while this cacophony of mockingbirdese continued outside.

Now, the windows were closed. The Bradford pear where our warbling, fine-feathered friend was on stage was about 20 feet from the window. We even shut the door to the bathroom which was between the bedroom and the tree outside. We could still hear this dude over the humming of the air conditioning.

It occurred to me that this was a young, misguided teenbird, "playing" his music at number 10 decibel while cruising the neighborhood. What kind of bird parents would allow this? What kind of bird family values must this bird have? Where was Dan Bird Quayle when I needed him? Somewhere in Indiana I guess but that's another story.

Finally, I decided to go to the source. The tree. In my P's – summer version of my PJ's – I walked to the door, down the steps, and up to the tree. At 3:00a.m., mind you, in my neighborhood with various outdoor spotlights lighting my way, standing in my P's, I grabbed several limbs and gave 'em a shake. "Go home, you stupid bird," I hollered, "I'm trying to sleep!"

I heard nothing and, thinking I had scared it off, returned to my bed. Well, of course, it came back, and it was at that point, my shotgun appeared in my "night vision." For a fleeting moment, I considered the possibility. But I could also visualize the headline TV news the next day…"Man goes berserk…shoots up his own Bradford pear tree in the middle of the night…with nothing on but his P's…neighbors say he seemed like a nice guy…"

Sometime after 4 or 5 in the morning, I finally drifted back to sleep. For some reason, it was gone the next night and never seemed to bother us thereafter. Honest, I'm not making this up.

If I didn't know better, I would have thought this might be a new version of another old movie by Alfred Hitchcock, entitled The Bird.

THE YELLOW
"GOOBIE DUST" IS A
PERIL TO THE NOSTRILS

Ah, springtime in Atlanta. It is a gorgeous experience. Snifff. The azaleas are beautimous and the - AAAHHH-chewww – dogwoods are bright with their stately white pedals.

I don't know how it happened, but God in His infinite wisdom has done a great thing – Keerrr-spleeww – by creating the right climate, rainfall, sunshine, and various pungent fertilizers to infiltrate the roots and shoots, so that we could be the grateful recipients of such a wonder – Ah, ahmmmiiiffff – ful sight on the earth which – Aah, aah, aahhhh,blouiiii - messes up my nose, er, I mean, brings joy of His creation.

As you know, though, - hghyyke-pptouii – we have to take a little bad…addd-chooo – with the good…golly, where's the kleenex. You know, for every action there's a re – CHEWWW – action.

And so, with the spring of floral beauty, there comes the dreaded, anthophobic, (this is a fear of flowers – not that I fear them, but to use the expression, they "mess with my head") - Yellow Hy…Hyy…Hypodermia…floouuiiieee! If you have ever lived in Georgia, you know that the hideous Y.H. bursts forth from the lobb-lollipop pine trees around April Fool's Day – a "day which lives in inflorality" – and covers as well as infiltrates any and everything in it's wake…blooonnnnkkk, bloonnbkkk!

This has been going on probably since the beginning of Hybiscus-sed Period, soon after the capture of Geronimo the Germinator. The issue worsened because of the cross-pollination and polluting among bumble bees, causing us to be more cross as well as pollinated in the process.

Some people today are so - arre, arr, arrrre, splewww – convoluted over it that their doctors will not let them come out of the house all year, except on Groundhog Day, in which case, if they see their shadow, they sneeze, honk, and snort for six weeks prior to the April 1 germination...ex, ex, exploooooosionnnn!

As you can tell already, this writer is so effected – snifff – that I have a hard time thinking co...co...ooohhh, aaahhhh spuuueee...herently on the subject in question, the Yellow Hypodermia, or, as I call it, "goobie dust." It covers everything imaginable for weeks. Gets on your nose, in your nose, in your ears, in your navel. Awful!

Every day, some news person greets us with the pollen – aaah, aaah, flouieee – count which sometimes goes as high as 2500. I don't know what that means, unless it indicates the number of times you sneeze each day.

Now, I hasten to say that I've had much experience sneezing since my "up-bringing" days in western Kentucky where I – iiiIII-shoouuu – grew up. There was the ghastly Ambrosia A. Artemisiifolia that I had to contend with. I'm not making this up! This is commonly known as the repugnant ragweed, king of the great "AAAHHH – SCHLOUEEWWW" among allergy sufferers.

Nothing would make my life more miserable in the late summer and early fall than the A.A. Artemisiifolia, or ragweed. My nose would run for weeks, snnniffff. My mother tried to console me, as I snorted and sneezed horridly, letting me know that it was "in the genes," because noses ran in my family. But mine ran ahead of everyone else's.

So, I - honk, honk, honk – "nose" what others are going through in the spring. It's a plague. I've had shots, pills, syrups, remedies, examinations by nose doctors, throat doctors, cough doctors, and sneeze doctors. Nothing has ever worked. Even the instructions don't make sense..."take one pill three times a day." You can't do that.

And, as I mentioned at the very first essay of this book, springtime is a time for big "slurpy" smooches with your best sweetie and not k-blooouuie sniffffies all over your best sweetie. 'Cause when your nose is running freely, well, it can be embarrassing.

Which reminds me of a verse from the Pollen Blues...

When I was just sixteen, I took the Rutabagas Queen
    to the Christian County Fair.
We were dancin' real close, when I noticed that my nose, was
    drippin' on her auburn hair.
I looked kinda lanky, as I reached for my hanky,
    while I sneezed a dozen time or more,
She got tired of waitin', grabbed the bus back to Trenton,
    left me sniffin' all alone on the floor.

Like I say…embarrassing!

SUFFERING FROM THE SOUND OF TOO MUCH SILENCE

There's a place below the "gnat line" on the other side of Tifton, Georgia called Norman Park. (See "small" in the dictionary).

Maybe they should have called it Norman Baptist Park, because Baptists, mostly, are acquainted with it. One of the two state Baptist Conference centers is located there. It used to be a small Baptist college until, like so many denominational schools of its size, it went "de-funk, due to lack of de-funds."

Back in the 90s, I would be asked to participate in conferences with Baptist groups which involved conferences, "preachings," and lots of fellowship, a thing invented by Baptists a thousand years ago when they didn't have conferences and they just, well, had fellowship.

On one visit, I was asked to bring the entertainment for an alumni group of former "Normanites," as they called themselves. After the program, I stayed overnight while most of the folks left. Not to speak disparagingly of this little hamlet, but "I spent a week in Norman Park, Georgia that night." (There's a good country song there, huh?)

The dinner and program were over around 8p.m. and I was in my room by about 8:30, because there was no "planned" fellowship with the group, and no further "nightlife" in the metropolis of beautiful downtown Norman Park. (See "small" above.)

The room provided for me at the conference center was adequate for my needs, but in the true Baptist sense, it gave the term "generic" a new meaning. Bed, dresser with mirror, table with two chairs, small table with lamp by the bed, commode, basin, shower with two match-book size bars of soap, running water, towel, and washcloth. That was it.

No radio. No television. No "SuperVision." No telephone. No digital clock. No 2-cup coffee pot. No remote control by the bed. No booklet about night life in downtown Norman Park. No menu for continental breakfasts. No mints on my pillow.

In fact, there wasn't even a picture on the wall, which after awhile, I began to stare at. Ever been so bored in a room that you just stared at the wall? I began to sing the old Feron Young country song, "Hello, Walls."

Basically, what this scenario brought to mind is how blank our mind becomes when there is no TV, radio, telephone, or VCR. When there is no ball game or favorite TV show to watch. When there is no talk show to tune in to nor music to listen to. No way to call anyone and talk up a storm.

Guess I could have written a letter – a vanishing art in our culture nowadays - but I brought no paper. Same for a book or magazine. Just didn't think about it. And, of course, my body is programmed not to begin sleeping until around 11:00 or so. It was, and is, a dilemma for us busy persons, this room, void of our familiar gadgets. We have come to subsist on these trinkets of the world. It can almost produce a panic attack if we don't have them at our fingertips.

However, one thing came to mind there in downtown Norman Park, as I wall-watched, twiddled my thumbs, and contemplated the origin of the dreadful, floral drapes against the light salmon wall.

And that was, the serendipitous experience of *silence*. I suppose if you experience to much of "The Sound of Silence," the old Simon & Garfunkel tune title, you might go slightly batty. But for a time, even two very short hours before retiring, it can become a precious commodity in this crazy, loud, and many times, offensive world we live in.

Equally serendipitous was something else I found, after about an hour of my contemplative silence. Below the lamp, on the shelf of the table by my bed, stuck in the back corner, I found a Gideon's Bible. Baptists and the Gideons have blended well through the years, when it occurs to me that very little seems to blend with Baptists now.

So, for the next little while, I found that I was comforted further in my unfamiliar "sound of silence." Sometimes silence is loathesome. Sometimes, even in beautiful downtown Norman Park, silence is golden. We could use more of it.

GOING TO THE EDGE
FOR A DIFFERENT VIEW

A world away, at edge of sand, live two creations by the sand, Divergent, while in proximity, they teach to all what all should see. (from poem, "Where Ocean Mist Meets City Breath" by JM)

If you've ever been to the western "edge," you can't help but see God's unique creation where the ocean meets land. I have been there several times over the past 25 years. Son, Scott, and his family are ensconced in the city of Santa Cruz, located on the northern tip of Monterey Bay.

We were there when the precursor of the '89 earthquake shook us out of our bed one night in August. The big one came two months later and we were glad we were back in Atlanta at the time. The Santa Cruz family faired o.k., with only jangled nerves.

I returned for more visits through the 90s and during an afternoon of one such trip, I traveled alone out to a roadside park on the outskirts of Santa Cruz at the water's edge. Along the road there was a "turnout" now and then – a place for sitting, looking, strolling, biking, or just to pause and contemplate, if you like.

I discovered one "turnout" that was jutting out toward the ocean farther than most others along the winding drive. I pulled in and parked. A path led toward the ocean to the point and came to an abrupt end with a well-placed, flat rock about two feet wide. That was as far as you could go, with a 30 foot or so drop-off where the water splashes wildly against the rocks below. It was literally, the cliff's edge.

Well, somewhat characteristically of course, I wanted to go as far as I could and this flat rock was it. There, I planted my feet and stood with a bit of defiance, facing the northwest wind – hair blowing, trousers flapping, as nature blew its force in my direction, ever-pushing toward the city behind me. I stared at the rocky edge below as the ocean waves rolled in furiously, fed by the onrushing wind.

Momentarily, a thought hit me – one which was made popular by ole Forrest Gump. "Stupid is as stupid does!" he would say.

I began to think that it was a bit stupid to stand this close, and if I "does" continue, I could fall, especially if the wind changes, and I would be a "stupid" as well as sorry sucker then.

I bowed to sensibility and slowly moved back to the safety of an appropriate bench a few feet away and sat awhile, enjoying the view. Most people with half a brain would have thought me crazy to get so close. My dear wife would have screamed bloody murder. I could slip, lose my footing, etc., etc. So, my "cooler" head prevailed.

While seated at the bench, basking in the warm breezes, and looking out toward the vast "end" of the ocean on the horizon miles away, I "thunk" to myself. While in my dream-state, I glanced over a few feet away and noticed the words of a strategically placed sign, not far from the flat rock in question.

"Warning!" it stated. *"Cliff Edges Are Dangerous. Unstable Cliffs, High Water, And Slipper Rocks Can Badly Injure You. Remember! Hazardous And Changing Conditions May Exist. Be Cautious – Play Safe!"*

Is there a more foreboding message within the commentaries of life, I ask? More and more in this culture of ours, we hear words of caution…Warning! Philosophers may be dangerous! High theologians, orators, physicians, or politicians may be slippery! Even the voice of the computer which is connected to our automobile gas gauge says "Warning, you've gone about as far as you can go!"

Perhaps it might have been prudent for God to have placed a similar sign in the Garden of Eden for Adam and Eve. "Warning! Forbidden fruit ahead! Snake may be deceiving. Be cautious, play safe." May not have mattered to Eve…Adam either.

Sure, the bench was safe and I sat there and continued to get the feel of the ocean, the breeze, the sun and waves. But it wasn't like standing on that rock out there at the point. There, you experience more than just "the feel of the ocean." You get the exhilaration. It's a different view…you're really there.

So, I sat until the sun was about to set in the west. Then, I stood, ready to head back to my son's place. I looked out over the water and paused. You would know it. I walked back to the rock and stood momentarily, one more time, feeling a bit of triumph.

STEPPING BACK IN TIME WITH OLD(ER) FRIENDS

In my opinion, one of God's most ingenious works of art within us humans is the memory. And one of the most joyful activities in the latter years of one's life is sharing with long-time friends the memories you both experienced.

Such is the case at a class reunion. In '93, I attended my first one – the 40th. And to paraphrase Paul Harvey, "now you know the rest of my age." Bring on the prune juice and let's have a toast.

If you've been to one late in life, you know that feelings are multiple. Some are natural, some are difficult to describe, others are personal and mostly nobody's business. Not all memories are pleasant. But on the reunion occasions, you stay positive.

First off, just trying to grasp the fact that forty years have passed since you laid eyes on some of these guys and gals is startling enough. How do you share a lifetime of "water over the dam," detours traveled, and cataclysmic events of agony or ecstasy? Well, you don't. You know you can't do much more than hit the high spots.

So the ritual begins, this "rite of passage" for the constantly aging, and you step through the doors of the rented clubhouse and back in time, forty years before…to a world you remembered mainly by face…even though broader, or thinner, or more wrinkled, or rearranged by facial hair.

You put yourself on "auto pilot" and deal with the obligatory questions…Where do you live, tell me about your family, what kind of work do you do, are you retired yet, what ever happened to your little brother? Unless you've been close to one another through the years, you hardly get a chance to do more than a handshake, a hug, give the barest of details, then glance over the room toward another and repeat the process.

You tell some people they have hardly changed, and others how good they look, and still others that you are embarrassed you didn't recognize them. In some cases, you lie through your teeth, trying to maintain composure at what you see, and in other cases, you just blurt out, as one did to me…"Gawd all mighty, Joe, what happened to your hair?"

But now, it's okay. You know you're accepted for what you were 40 years ago and 40 years hence. And everyone accepts the ribbing and we're happy to see those who were able to be there, sad to learn of some who couldn't make it, and then grieve, albeit briefly, to learn of those who never will again.

"In my little town," to borrow the first line of an old Paul Simon tune, the streets are filled with memories. Most of my classmates grew up "down the street and around the corner" from each other. From three grade schools, we converged our lives for five years at "Hoptown High" – the only high school in the city limits – and struggled through "Beowolf" in Miss Vaughn's English class, memorized all the dates in Mr. Gough's history class, cheered for a less-than-average football team, cried when a better-than- average basketball team got beat in the finals. Some loved and lost, some loved and won. It all culminated one May night of 1953…when I was 17…it was a very good year.

Our name was called, and one by one, we stood and paraded across the stage, received our degree from our principal, Mr. Charlie Petrie, the little Scotsman, turned back to our seat, and it was over. Actually, it was just beginning, but we were too dumb or dumbfounded to know it. I look back over those years and wonder if I ever did realize when "it began."

And so, we now find ourselves, hunkered down at a table, eating and sharing as much as we can within the time frame. Two nights together, maybe just one, and it's "back to the reality" of present-day living either in this small western Kentucky town, or some "timbuktu" in another state.

Time is cruel. It keeps running out. It made the reunion bare-ly a "re-connection." But a brief connection is better than no connection. It reminded us of the "union" we once had, and even now, with a little effort, might rekindle to some extent. Lord, honey, in the blink of an eye, it'll be a 50-year reunion.

A LITTLE "REVIVING" IS GOOD FOR THE SOUL

"The law of the Lord is perfect, reviving the soul."
Psalms 19:7

As one who is a *believer*, as well as a minister for lo, these many years, I can think of no one who could "revive the soul" through the perfect law of the Lord than one Billy Graham.

In the mid-nineties, Billy Graham brought one of his patented crusades to Atlanta. Slow of gate, but still the ever-capturing preacher, he said he would "keep on preaching until the Lord retires me." It was my good fortune to hear him in person one more time.

The first time I heard Billy Graham was at a big revival during my early college days back in the mid-fifties. A busload of young people went over from western Kentucky to the Vanderbilt stadium in Nashville, Tennessee. I never saw so many people at a "preaching" in my life, up to then.

In Atlanta, he attempted to "revive our soul" in the Georgia Dome. You could put several stadiums in that thing, as well as four or five home towns. I was glad to be a part of the crowd whose souls were stirred to hear this "man of God for all seasons."

I don't know when Billy Graham started preaching, probably before the World War II. That's over a half century of admonishing folks to "get right with God." And no one that I have ever heard, either in person or on television, has ever come close to his ability, easy candor, and straight-forward, no-nonsense way of presenting the good gospel.

I met him once. He has a good handshake. My dad used to say you could trust a preacher with a good handshake. Admittedly, there are some preachers I wouldn't trust any further than I could throw a train. Billy Graham, I trust.

I've been to a lot of revival meetings in my lifetime. Some were foot-tapping, some were dull. Some revived the spirits of people who didn't know they had spirits, and some wouldn't have revived a nanny goat.

101

Believe it or not, I even helped lead a couple myself. During my seminary days, I led the "sangin'" for a revival at the Bethabra Baptist Church of Habit, Kentucky. True! My friend, "Bull Moose" Marshall was the preacher. A crusty ole football player and ex-marine, his spirit "got tackled" as a junior in college and he decided to preach. What I remember most was the food prepared each day for the visiting preacher and song leader. I would say, many a piece of chicken "entered the ministry" on that adventure. It was "dinner," not lunch, and there were huge amounts. A different farm each day!

My "revivaling" didn't last long after that. One night an old gentleman came up and said, "Brother Joe, you're goin' a long way in music, 'cause if you stay in music, you're gonna to have to go a long, long way." I heeded his advice, as those who've heard me sing would appreciate.

I don't know what the word "revival" conjures up in your mind. Maybe snake handling in an eastern Kentucky church house in the hills. Maybe the old movie, "Elmer Gantry" or the newer movie, "The Apostle." Or maybe Billy Graham's crusades, beamed by television around the world.

The term, as well as the style, may be passe` to much of our culture today. But whether or not, we all need reviving from time to time. Perhaps our families need reviving, our communities need reviving, or perhaps your own spirit needs to be revived toward that which is "kinder and gentler," to quote a famous Bush of old.

Regardless of your religious persuasion, "revival" itself may be the religion each of us needs. It could be found in the smile of your grandchild, the "A" you received on a test, or the help offered by a concerned neighbor. Reviving may come from different directions, even from reading this book, if I may take presumptuous liberties.

By the time you read this, I hope Billy Graham is still preaching to revive the soul of our world in the 21st century. And when the Good Lord chooses to "take him up," I feel confident He will soon raise another up to carry the great "reviving banner."

Selah!

EPILOGUE

Beyond the nines

So, adios to the "nines"…from 1900 to 1999, we have observed, experienced, or read about probably the most significant millennium of all creation. During these 100 years, life as we know it in the "U. S. of A." has, in the eyes of the "average Joe," and Josephine, changed immeasurably…from riding a horse to the barn, to riding a shuttle beyond the moon…from wearing spats to church to wearing flip-flops to a wedding…from the "um-pa" of the John Philip Sousa band to the nasal twang of the Willie Nelson band…from the telephone on the wall to a cell phone in your pocket!

A speaking of the telephone, well, some things never change. We were talking on the phone in 1900, albeit in archaic fashion by "ringing up central." And we're still talking on the telephone, albeit this time with the infamous cell model, "smaller than a bread box," or slice of bread in the box, for that matter. But for the 21st century, I have a telephone theory. Permit me to elaborate on this electronic change.

It is my belief that in the very near future, we will be able to purchase – possibly even "over the counter" – a small, yea, teensy phone chip which may be "installed" in our ear, as easily as, say, a boy's ear ring…which will be activated to the Big Phone satellite-in-the-sky, and will ring in your ear when someone calls and all you have to do to answer it is pull on your earlobe and start talking.

Advantages? No more phones to carry in your purse, install in your bathroom, or hang on your belt like Clint Eastwood's "make my day," 357 magnum. Then, when you are driving, your hands will be free at last, free at last, mainly to hold your hamburger, eye liner, and road map! Okay, so it's just a theory. It may need some work.

"And now, the end has come," as the late Frank Sinatra warbled, and my trilogy of Mason Jar writings has concluded. And I have retired from my gainful employment of the 1960-1999 years in ministry. It is the 21st century and I made it to 2000A.D. and a bit beyond, and am receiving "free" money from the government. So what is there left to say...? Well, I give you a poem of "life in the frog lane."

It seems most appropriate for me to include this poem because of it's philosophy. It is of utmost importance for a frog *not* to forget his ability to keep hopping. Or in this case, "kicking." And it's a serious thing for us humans not to forget to keep on kickin', as well. Hopefully, this may give you appropriate, poetic incentive.

I do not know who composed this poem, but many have used it before me, and many will use it after. And I have used it in between. I first discovered this versed philosophy at a recreation conference at Ridgecrest, North Carolina, circa 1963. To be thoroughly editorial and give credit where credit is due, I should admit that it is was written by "Author Unknown," may he or she rest in peace. And so, herewith...

THE SAGA OF THE TWO FROGS

Two young frogs from inland bogs had spent a night a-drinking.
As morning broke and they awoke, while yet their eyes were
    blinking,
The farmer's pail came to the swale and caught them quick as
    winking.

Ere they could gather scattered senses, or breath a prayer for past
    offenses,
The farmer, quick fast-working man had scooped them up for the
    milkman's can.
The can filled up, the lid went down, and soon those frogs were
    off to town.

The luckless frogs began to quake and sober up in cold milk-
    shake.
They fear that life will surely stop if they don't swim up to the top.
They kick and swim and kick and swim until their poor ole eyes
    grow dim.

"Say there, ole top," said one poor sport, "I can no longer hold
the fort."

"I've no more kick in life, why try it? I wasn't raised on a fresh
milk diet."

"Tut-tut, my lad," the other cried. "A frog's not dead until he's
died."

"Keep on kicking, that's my plan. We may yet see outside this
can!"

"No use, no use," the first frog sighed, turned up his toes and
gently died.

The other frog, undaunted still, kept on kicking with a right good
will,

Until with joy to great to utter, he found he'd churned a pound of
butter.

And climbing on that bit of grease, he slid off to town with the
greatest of ease.

So...

When life is tough and gets you down, and you wonder why you
have a frown,

Just keep on kicking, don't get in a flutter,

One more kick might bring your butter!

Author Unknown

* * * * * * *

So...keep on kickin'!

Joe Mason